First Contact

First Contact

Teaching and Learning in Introductory Sociology

Nancy A. Greenwood and Jay R. Howard

ROWMAN & LITTLEFIELD PUBLISHERS, INC.
Lanham • Boulder • New York • Toronto • Plymouth, UK

Published by Rowman & Littlefield Publishers, Inc.
A wholly owned subsidiary of The Rowman & Littlefield Publishing Group, Inc.
4501 Forbes Boulevard, Suite 200, Lanham, Maryland 20706
http://www.rowmanlittlefield.com

Estover Road, Plymouth PL6 7PY, United Kingdom

British Library Cataloguing in Publication Information Available

Library of Congress Cataloging-in-Publication Data

Greenwood, Nancy A.
  First contact : teaching and learning in introductory sociology / Nancy A.
Greenwood and Jay R. Howard.
    p. cm.
  Includes bibliographical references.
  ISBN 978-0-7425-2897-0 (cloth : alk. paper) — ISBN 978-0-7425-2898-7
(pbk. : alk. paper) — ISBN 978-1-4422-1238-1 (electronic)
  1. Sociology—Study and teaching. I. Howard, Jay R. II. Title.
HM571.G746 2011
301—dc22   2011006786

♾™ The paper used in this publication meets the minimum requirements of
American National Standard for Information Sciences—Permanence of Paper
for Printed Library Materials, ANSI/NISO Z39.48-1992.

Printed in the United States of America

~

Contents

~

Acknowledgments

Being a teacher-scholar in sociology is an important part of my professional identity, and I have many people who have helped me to become a teacher-scholar and helped with this project. I was very fortunate both as an undergraduate and graduate student to have wonderful role models who were teacher-scholars. They are Dean S. Dorn at California State University, Sacramento, and the late Joe DiMartini formerly at Washington State University. They both encouraged involvement in teaching-related activities and nurtured me as a teacher-scholar.

Countless colleagues at Indiana University, Kokomo have aided me. Nadene Keene, Sue Ridlin, and Sue Sciame Giesecke read early versions of the book prospectus and the first chapter, offering many helpful suggestions. Other colleagues including Angela Becker, Julie Saam, and Karla Farmer Stouse have helped indirectly by creating a context where teacher-scholars could grow and be supported. I am grateful, also, for the assistance that Indiana University, Kokomo has provided via funding for Summer Faculty Fellowships and sabbatical leave which helped support the writing of this book.

I am indebted to my colleagues in the Midwest Sociological Society, the Section on Teaching and Learning in Sociology of the American Sociological Association, and especially the Departmental Resources Group of the American Sociological Association for countless sessions, articles, books, presentations, and informal conversations about teaching in general and teaching introductory sociology in particular. Those who have been particularly supportive and helpful at various times include Diane Pike (who reviewed early drafts of several chapters), Carol A. Jenkins, Kathleen McKinney, Edward Kain, and Jeanne Ballantine. Most of all, I am grateful for the collaboration of my coauthor, Jay Howard, whose many contributions helped bring this book to completion. Jay's work ethic, his dedication to teaching, learning, and SoTL research, and his long-time colleagueship made him the right choice for coauthor. I would be remiss if I did not acknowledge the leadership and guidance of the late Carla Howery. Carla would sometimes kiddingly call me the "Intro Guru"; coming from her, it was great praise and gave me the confidence I needed to write. We also want to thank Sarah Stanton, Della Vache, Jin Yu, and others at Roman & Littlefield for their assistance with the editing and production of this book. Thanks also to Robert A. Saigh for his help with the indexing. Both Jay and I are also grateful to the four anonymous reviewers whose comments were invaluable to improving our final draft. Finally, and most importantly, I could not do this work without the love, patience, support, and understanding of both my wonderful husband and partner, Michael V. Hickman, and my amazing daughter, Mikael Anne Greenwood-Hickman.

Nancy A. Greenwood, January 2011

I want to recognize the many colleagues who have contributed to my development as a teacher-scholar including those at IUPUC and IUPUI as well as colleagues throughout the Indiana University system, particularly those members of the Faculty Colloquium for Excellence in Teaching (FACET) who annually come together to talk about teaching and challenge each other in the pursuit of greater student learning. In particular, I wish to acknowledge the mentoring influence of the late Eileen Bender, who as the first FACET director saw something in me while I was still a new Assistant Professor and actively nurtured that potential. I am also appreciative of my many new colleagues at Butler University, particularly in the College of Liberal Arts and Sciences who have already begun to involve me in similar discussions about teaching and learning! And I must recognize the administrative assistants at IUPUC and Butler who have kept me in line and on track, Vicki Kruse and Priscilla Cobb.

I am deeply indebted to my many professional colleagues in sociology, particularly those active in the teaching movement through the North Central Sociological Association and the American Sociological Association's Section on Teaching and Learning in Sociology. Foremost among these is my coauthor, Nancy Greenwood, who graciously invited me to join her in this project after she already had it well under way. Like Nancy, I too am deeply indebted to the late Carla Howery for her leadership and mentoring! And I would be remiss if I did not thank my undergraduate and graduate mentors at Indiana University, South Bend and the University of Notre Dame who helped spark the sociological imagination in me and a love for teaching and learning sociology. Finally, I would like to thank my wife, Brenda, and my children, Amalia and Dylan, for their love, patience, and support.

Jay Howard, August 2010

CHAPTER ONE

~

Rethinking Introductory Sociology

"In today's rapidly changing world, a few things seem not to change much, if at all. One of these is the widespread dissatisfaction of sociologists with the introductory course . . . radical surgery is indicated and the best hope for the introductory course lies in major overhaul" (Lenski 1985: 101). In his paper about rethinking introductory sociology, Gerhard Lenski describes a three-part introduction to sociology with courses devoted to macro-, meso-, and microsociological domains, each with a strong historical/comparative emphasis. While Lenski's historical/ comparative approach to introductory sociology never enjoyed the central importance and popularity that Lenski would have liked, his rationale for advocating change in this course is still pertinent today. He suggests that introductory students "are confronted with dozens of definitions and countless scraps and bits of information of this subject and that, but they can never discover a unifying core to the discipline which establishes the intellectual relevance and relationships of the component parts" (Lenski 1985: 103). Lenski further argues that an even more serious problem is that students "get no sense of sociology as a discipline concerned with important and challenging *intellectual* problems" (Lenski 1985: 103). Where have we heard this before? Lenski wrote this more than 25 years ago, yet we still continue to hear these kinds of statements from our colleagues today.

We have written this book to examine such complaints and to address issues which may appear to be unrelated to what we do and teach in this course. We will suggest that there should be a good fit between course design and course goals with the broader institutional context and mission. We will explain why it is important to know who your students are and how this influences course design. We will present research and discuss the most common tools of the trade including selecting a textbook and constructing a syllabus. We present an overview of the literature on designing and delivering effective lectures, leading better discussions, and assessing what your students know. Finally, we provide faculty development suggestions and resources for ongoing enhancement of both teacher and student learning. We hope to provide the tools needed for building great introductory sociology courses and to provoke greater discussion among our colleagues about how we can improve introductory sociology courses.

Introductory Sociology Today

In the journal *Teaching Sociology*, over forty articles and teaching notes were published between 1985 and 2009 offering advice and guidance specifically for the introductory sociology course. While there has been a plethora of materials published to help us teach this course, we have only begun to define discipline-specific standards for introductory sociology. Thus, teacher-scholars in sociology have a substantial body of literature, in both *Teaching Sociology* and teaching resource sets published by the American Sociological Association (ASA), available for them to use in designing and teaching courses and helping students learn sociology that were simply not available thirty years ago. The availability of these resources for teaching and learning is particularly helpful because we are called to take on many roles that often take away time from this important task!

In higher educational contexts full-time college and university professors as well as part-time faculty and graduate assistants who teach sociology are asked to wear many hats in addition to that of teacher. We are often also researchers, advisors, mentors to students and colleagues, administrators, committee members, committee chairpersons, computer software users, and even recruiters of new students to their schools and/or to the major. In addition to academic duties, teachers also have personal lives with family and community commitments. With so many hats to wear, by necessity we build efficient daily routines which help us to perform these tasks and meet all of these various expectations and deal with the stresses of role conflict and role strain in our lives. Time is precious to us all and sometimes the longer we teach the more precious it becomes. Semester after semester and sometimes year after year may pass by and we find ourselves following the path of least resistance and teaching sociology much in the same ways we did years earlier. Moreover, instructors often adopt the same book or kinds of books year after year with little or no discussion among colleagues of how sociology ought to be presented, could be presented, or of how sociology fits into the campus's general education curriculum. We wonder if too often we adapt our teaching and our course to the textbook in the same way students are expected to adapt to it as they read and study its content. How often do we have the luxury of taking time to stop, reflect, and ask ourselves, "How could we do this better? How could we better demonstrate to students how important or useful sociological insight and information is?" Reading this book will provide you with opportunities to do just that.

The Path of the Teacher-Scholar

But what is *better teaching* . . . better than what? Is *better teaching* covering more material, that is, more content? Does *better* mean having students get better grades? Does better teaching mean using flashy PowerPoint presentations or personal response systems (e.g., clickers)? Does *better* mean getting improved course evaluations of your teaching? Yes, *better* could mean all of these. At the same time, wouldn't it be *better* if students in our introductory sociology classes mastered a few important sociological concepts, understood why they are important and useful, and were able to grasp sociology's science and empiricism by looking at what has been studied? Wouldn't it be *better* if students completed the course with the ability to use sociological theories and concepts? Wouldn't it be *better* if they could use them to understand their own experiences in society? *Better* can also mean helping students to develop the ability to take sociological perspectives, use them, and, in some small or great way, to change society.

The approach we take in this book to improve teaching and learning is to ground what we do in the scholarship of teaching and learning (SoTL). McKinney argues that it is important to distinguish between good teaching, scholarly teaching, and the scholarship of teaching and learning (2004). She defines *good teaching* as "that which promotes student learning and other desired student outcomes" (McKinney et al. 2004: 8). Good teaching also supports program, departmental, and institutional goals and objectives. On the other hand, *scholarly teaching*, according to McKinney, goes beyond good teaching in that it involves taking the same approach to teaching that we take in our substantive areas of expertise. Scholarly teachers are reflexive; they use assessment data and other sources in systematic course design. They are risk takers and are willing to try new techniques. They discuss pedagogy with colleagues and, most importantly, they "read and apply the literature on teaching and learning in their discipline" (McKinney et al. 2004: 8). Finally, *the scholarship of teaching and learning* includes research, presentation, and publication of systematic assessments of teaching and learning. It includes published research about teaching and learning. We advocate good teaching, scholarly teaching, *and* the use of SoTL research for the development of excellence in teaching and learning. We hope that some readers will continue conducting or begin to conduct investigations into their own teaching and students' learning and share these with other scholars.

The *best practices* approach to the scholarship of teaching and learning has become a common mechanism for sharing insightful and new ways to teach and provide students with opportunities to learn. (See Chickering and Gamson 1987.) This approach is used in this book as a way to share models of teaching and learning when constructing a syllabus, selecting a text or reading material, and thinking about modes of information delivery and presentation, as well as for student assignments and activities designed to promote student learning. We identify *best practices* where they can be found in the literature throughout this book and construct them where they are not found to offer alternative and/or new strategies for teaching and learning in sociology.

It is a fair assumption that most instructors want to see students succeed in the introductory course. They want to engage students with sociology, and most instructors likely feel that they are, at least in part, responsible for that engagement. Students today are very diverse in social background characteristics, in academic preparedness, and in worldly experiences. While we really do not have many studies about the long- or short-term impact of introductory sociology on students, there are some data about the extent to which we meet students' expectations. Gigliotti (1987) argues that students generally do not have negative views of introductory sociology. If this is so, how can we help them leave with useful information? What impact should introductory sociology have on our students? What do we want them to learn and why? We will explore how we might do a better job of teaching our students and helping them learn what we believe is so important about sociology.

In this book we want to ask questions that require us to use *our own* sociological imaginations to improve our teaching and students' learning. We can reflect about teaching and consider how students' biographies might connect with their larger social contexts. This book will provide instructors with such opportunities for reflection. We believe that many sociology instructors have unmet expectations about what they would like to have their students accomplish. Some sociology instructors have not developed carefully articulated expectations for their students and the introductory course. Instructors often have not discussed these expectations with others who teach the same courses. In this book we look at the extent to which, as a discipline, we have consensus about what we want our courses to include. We ask whether we are meeting our own expectations for what this course should be. Are we meeting our expectations for what this course *could* be? In this book, we hope to explore these issues and to bring them into the public venue for more discussion.

Knowing Our Students

Good pedagogy has long suggested that we know our publics, but it is especially important for teachers to know their students. Not only can we identify the demographic characteristics of students at our own universities, but we can also learn much about the student subcultures as well as the individuals in our classes. The bottom line is that you can teach more effectively to those whom you know because you have a better sense of what they need. Armed with this information, one can design a course to better fit one's audience or public. Only then can we offer learning opportunities that make sociology relevant to them as adults and citizens in today's world.

Today's traditional-aged college students are very tech-savvy, have been reared on a diet of Sesame Street short-attention-span snippets, and have expectations that our classrooms should be as dazzling as the Disney experience. But not all of us teach traditional-aged students, and many of us teach first-generation college students. College students come from a diverse set of international, subcultural, and religious backgrounds. They have many characteristics, qualities, and behaviors that students in the past have not. As sociologists we are experts about diversity. We should recognize that not only are students diverse, so are academic institutions. The differentiation of academic institutions is perhaps the single most salient feature of American higher education (Calhoun 1999: 25). Therefore, if we want to facilitate student learning, it is critical that we take seriously differences in these contexts and understand our students, their needs, and their abilities.

At the same time we must recognize that most students enter college and introductory sociology courses with a psychological-individualistic bias in their view of the world. The causes of human behavior are most often judged by them to be nearly exclusively located within the individual. Students usually have not yet developed a sociological imagination that would allow them to see how social context and expectations often drive individual behavior and decisions. Instead, they readily assume the individual is always and virtually entirely responsible for his or her circumstances such as unemployment, deviance, or inequality. A significant challenge for faculty who teach introductory sociology courses is to get students to begin to question their psychological-individualistic views of the world and provide opportunities for them to see how individual choices are often constrained by social contexts. If we fail to develop students' appreciation for a sociological perspective in the introductory sociology course, those students may never learn to think sociologically. They may never understand the social forces that influence our world and our lives. Before we can do this, however, we must know who our students are, something about what they know, and figure out what we want them to learn. In this book we hope to convince sociology teachers that all students are not alike and help instructors find ways to get to know them.

Course Goals, Student Learning, and Assessment

It is not a new idea that college courses should be organized around a few stated objectives. This idea has been in the teaching literature for decades (Goldsmid 1980; Lewis 1995; Dominowski 2002). The guiding questions for setting objectives remain, "What do we want students to know about sociology?" and "What do we want our students to be able to do after completing the introductory sociology course?" Colleges, universities, and sociology programs often have published mission statements that can help determine the answer to this question. But it is also true that each instructor has the opportunity to provide his or her own emphasis. What is most important is that these goals should be thoughtfully constructed, likely in collaboration with departmental colleagues, and made explicit to students. What we want our students to learn and accomplish should not be a secret. Yet, it is so easy to forget to tell students and remind them often what it is we want them to learn. These objectives may be thought of as contractual statements between the instructor and student. They tell the student that the instructor is going to organize the course in such a way that these objectives can be achieved. This is a reasonable obligation for instructors to be expected to fulfill. This book asks questions to further discussion about goals and objectives so that faculty members can plan well and construct courses that meet programmatic goals and objectives.

Teaching that promotes student learning must begin with clearly defined goals that are obtainable and can be measured within the structure of a one-semester course which meets, traditionally, three hours a week. While most instructors have a few laudable goals for the introductory course listed on their syllabi, these are often vague and difficult to operationalize within any one course. One often-seen example is, "Students should develop a sociological imagination." While there is no argument that this is an important goal that could be part of any introductory sociology course, we also need to ask, how will opportunities to learn this ability be integrated into the course? What opportunities will students have to develop this ability? How will it be measured or evaluated?

What knowledge, skills, and abilities would you want students to have when the course is over? Once we have decided on what it is that we want students to learn and have written our goals and objectives, we also need to operationalize (to use our own jargon) those objectives into measurable student outcomes. This formal operationalization of objectives into measurable student behavioral outcomes is a relatively new idea in higher education. We explore the limitations and benefits of this process in a later chapter. We encourage instructors to ask, "What will students have to do, at what level will they need perform these tasks, in order to determine that the objectives have been met?" We offer suggestions about how we can best measure our students' successes and ultimately reflect on the teaching-learning environment we create in our classrooms.

We suggested above that course objectives in introductory sociology need to fit with the wider program and university goals. As sociologists we have the luxury of using our own conceptual tools to help students understand concepts such as organizational structure, social institutions, and how they work. In the chapters that follow we address the issues related to designing introductory sociology as a part of a general education curriculum, the curriculum of the major, and the extent to which consensus exists among sociology faculty about what should be in this course.

No model of teaching and learning is complete if it lacks an assessment component. Assessment of student learning is necessary to discover the extent to which both the teacher and student are successful at meeting course objectives, at measuring student outcomes, at understanding students' perceptions of the course experience, and for reflexively evaluating the program within which one teaches. Evaluation of student learning in any course should be tied to the learning goals and stated objectives for that course. Evaluation should not be a one-shot event. Students need to have opportunities to learn, but also practice using concepts before evaluation. Assessment of student learning is more useful if it is an ongoing process. We may also want to consider assessing the extent to which students have learned to apply the material to their own lives.

Assessment data are especially useful in improving one's own teaching. It is an important element in collecting data to support teaching effectiveness. Assessment provides the empirical data to support the effectiveness of an instructor's pedagogical strategies. Learning to incorporate assessment into the course design benefits both the instructor and the student. We will return to this subject in a later chapter and discuss some of the "best practices" in assessment and evaluation of student learning.

We wonder if it is also important that individual courses within and between campuses should share at least a few common goals for introductory sociology. Many sociology programs have adopted (or adapted some version of) the ASA's goals for the sociology major. (See *Liberal Learning and the Sociology Major*, Eberts et al. 1991 and *Liberal Learning and the Sociology Major Updated*, McKinney et al. 2004 for these goals.) While goals for *the major* have been established and revised in these two publications, there are no such universal standards *for introductory sociology* as a general education and/or a service course, let alone as the introduction to the major. This one course can contribute enormously to the liberal arts education of students and to general education goals. For this reason, it seems to be important to consider these for introductory sociology. While there may be many views about this, open discourse about such possible goals for the introductory course can only benefit sociology as well as our students.

Sociology and General Education

The ASA's Task Force on Sociology and General Education's report, *Sociology and General Education* (Keith et al. 2007) is an important document that helps frame what sociology has to offer the undergraduate student. At the broadest level, most sociology instructors want students to develop a wider perspective on the social world than the one they brought with them to college. Sociological theories and concepts help frame issues in a broader understanding of the social world in which we live. By gaining this broader understanding, students are better prepared to make informed, reasoned choices in their personal lives, families, careers, and communities. Sociology thereby helps prepare students to be civically engaged.

Unlike many other disciplines, we use multiple perspectives and theories when introducing sociology to students. This opportunity to compare and contrast perspectives typically comes much later in many disciplines, perhaps not until graduate study. By providing students with opportunities to examine social issues from a variety of perspectives, sociology offers a unique early experience in developing critical thinking skills, which is an often included goal of general education.

As we know, a sociological perspective is an alternative worldview to the typical psychological view of most freshman college students. Given the American emphasis on individualism, it is no surprise that college students frequently assume a psychological perspective and individualistic-based explanations for behavior. Sociology helps students see that while psychology is a valid social and behavioral discipline, not all human behavior is best understood in terms of individual attributes or personality. Sociology makes social patterns and social structure visible to students and it broadens their understanding of the factors that shape human behavior.

Over fifty years ago, C. Wright Mills (1959) wrote about the ability to see the connections between the individual and wider society. Most sociologists today agree that this is a central concept of our discipline. A key goal of the introductory sociology course therefore is often to help students begin to develop their sociological imaginations. By giving students multiple opportunities to see how individual experiences in society are shaped by wider social forces, we not only develop their sociological imaginations, but also provide a solid intellectual foundation for good citizenship in a democracy. If students understand why and toward what end their behavior matters, they will be more likely to become proactive, critically empowered members of society.

Another important habit of the mind that sociology offers students is the opportunity to learn how the scientific method can be employed to build a reasoned assessment of social problems. As students learn the rules of the scientific method as they are applied to social life, they develop the tools necessary to challenge taken-for-granted or commonsense understandings of social phenomena. They learn that opinion alone is not an explanation. Opinions need to be informed by data and evidence to create constructions of knowledge. Through sociology, students develop an appreciation for both qualitative and quantitative evidence as well as for the methodologies through which evidence is gathered. Developing a sociological imagination and learning to use a scholarly way of thinking about social issues are important components of most general education and/or sociology curricula.

Sociology is also uniquely situated in academe to provide students with intellectual capacities and skills that prepare them for the challenges they will confront throughout their lives. The ASA's Task Force on Sociology and General Education (Keith et al. 2007) also enumerated many of the ways in which sociology can contribute to the general education component of students' undergraduate studies:

1. Sociology illustrates the interplay between the macro and micro structures of the social world. Students learn that social forces and institutions influence the behavior of individuals while in turn being shaped and changed by such individuals.
2. Sociology demonstrates and explains the structured aspects of inequality. In today's world students often come to us with little or no understanding about "why racial and ethnic tensions persist" or "why some people are poor." Sociology offers explanations for these issues.
3. Sociology can describe, explain, and predict the properties of social groups. We know a lot about the structure of groups, including how status distinctions affect group decision making and organizational behavior.
4. Sociology demonstrates the importance of context in understanding social behavior. In addition to structural components, we can show how an understanding of social behavior must take into account spatial and temporal properties, including cultural contexts and dynamic processes.
5. Sociology enables students to see how they, as individuals, are connected to society. We talk about the self-concept, how it is different from the notion of personality, and how the self emerges in social context. We show how social roles develop and how the concept of the self changes over time. We demonstrate how

the self relates to social groups and how social groups affect the development and/or emergence of the self.

6. Sociology provides explanations of social change. In order to live and operate effectively within the twenty-first century, students need to have an appreciation for the dynamic interplay of social life. While changing rapidly, the world remains mired in tradition. Sociology provides students with insight about collective behavior, how social change occurs, the political and economic aspects of social change, as well as the barriers to social change. In this way, we help better prepare students to live and work in an ever-changing world, yet be aware of those aspects of society we might choose to preserve. (Keith et al. 2007: 13)

If it is a goal in introductory sociology courses to help students to take away the ability to make more informed decisions in their lives about family, work, and their roles in the community, then the habits of mind and special content of sociology are well suited to learn to do so. Our discipline offers students many perspectives on social issues, an array of critical thinking skills, and analytical frameworks for understanding society as well as a body of good information with which to make informed decisions. These are but a few examples of the wares we have to sell to our students. In this book we ask about the extent to which we do a good job of making these aspects of sociology clear to students. Do we clearly demonstrate to students in introductory sociology how to apply sociological knowledge to their own lives? When students satisfactorily complete an introductory sociology course, are we certain that they realize what sociology has to offer them? Have we sent students away with perspectives and information "in their back pocket" that they can then use in their lives? In this book we endeavor not only to help instructors consider the learning objectives of their courses and the extent to which they help students learn to use their sociological imaginations, but we also want to further a discussion within our discipline about what we teach in introductory sociology, about the extent to which there is consensus or no consensus about which concepts are central to our discipline, which concepts we should teach, and what students are actually learning.

Public Sociology in the Classroom

In his American Sociological Association's presidential address, Michael Burawoy stated that the challenge of public sociology "is to engage multiple publics in public ways" (Burawoy 2005: 4). It is not difficult to see teaching sociology as one way of "doing" public sociology. It may be the type of public sociology that has the most far-reaching arms and has the widest depth in terms of reaching the most people. The classroom is a very important venue where people learn what sociology is and what value it has for society. If it were not for that one introductory sociology course that many people take in college, they might not know what sociology is at all.

Earlier we addressed the various "hats" that sociology professors must wear. Professors and instructors of introductory courses wear *one more* hat we haven't yet mentioned. They might also think of themselves as ambassadors for our discipline. Introductory sociology instructors are students' *first contact* with sociology. Most of our students come to us with no experience with our area of study. This reality is the most challenging task of any to fulfill as an introductory sociology teacher. We must demonstrate to students what sociology means to their lives. If our classes bore students or make sociology seem dull and irrelevant to their lives, then we fail as sociological ambassadors. When this happens we also fail to initiate students to an exciting, useful, and insightful discipline that is very beneficial to their lives and communities. At the same time, when we as instructors fail at being good ambassadors, we lose the opportunity to help students develop a sociological imagination which they can take with them wherever their lives lead them. When we fail at this task, it also stands to reason that we fail to recruit students for upper-level courses, let alone majors or minors in sociology. What happens in introductory sociology is students' *first contact* with sociologists, but more importantly with sociology as a way of thinking about social reality.

Since the early 1990s scholars in sociology have talked about a public relations crisis in sociology. This crisis affects the role of the discipline of sociology in the broader academic community as well as the perceptions by the general public about our discipline. The extent of the work we have to do to improve the general public's perception of our discipline is evidenced in a column by humorist Dave Barry. While Barry targets the disciplines of English, philosophy, and psychology as well, he saves his sharpest barbs for sociology.

> For sheer lack of intelligibility, sociology is far and away the number one subject. I sat through hundreds of hours of sociology courses, and read gobs of sociology writing, and I never once heard or read a coherent statement. This is because sociologists want to be considered scientists, so they spend most of their time translating simple, obvious observations into scientific-sounding code. If you plan to major in sociology, you'll have to learn to do the same thing. For example, suppose you have observed that children cry when they fall down. You should write: "Methodological observation of the sociometrical behavior tendencies of prematurated isolates indicates that a causal relationship exists between groundward tropism and lachrimatory, or 'crying,' behavior forms." If you can keep this up for fifty or sixty pages, you will get a large government grant. (Barry 1993: 202–3)

This is a very harsh, if painfully humorous, view of sociology. Perhaps not everyone sees sociology this way, but outspoken voices such as Barry's have made this view popular. In the media we also sometimes see or hear public attacks on sociologists and their work. While the public impression of sociology has improved with the American Sociological Association's emphasis on public sociology, there is still much work for each of us to do. Barry's column speaks to the accessibility of sociological theory and research to our majors as well as to collateral majors such as those in psychology, anthropology, communications, nursing, criminal justice, and/or social work. Moreover, it points to the question of utility and relevance of sociology to the general educational core as our students see it connected to their work, their family lives, and their civic roles in the community.

From time to time we hear rumors among students or administrators that sociology is a dying discipline and its programs are being replaced by other, more applied or relevant disciplines such as social work or communication studies. While it is true that we have more competition for our courses and programs than in the past, sociologists know that what we do is different from what social workers do. While many of our students who graduate with bachelor's degrees in sociology compete with social work and psychology majors for entry-level positions in social service agencies, it is also true that sociological training provides them a unique point of view that can help them be better managers, supervisors, and even case workers in such organizations. Perhaps we have not done as good a job of sharing our knowledge about our discipline as we might do. Sociology is certainly not being replaced by other disciplines. It is alive and well and has much to offer both those who major in sociology and those in closely related fields. But it also has much to offer the student who takes only one course, the introductory course. It is our job as ambassadors of sociology to make sure our academic institutions and our local communities realize and understand what sociology offers our students. We think, too often, sociology undersells itself and/or presents itself in very unhelpful ways. One of the most important ways that we can be ambassadors for our discipline is by teaching introductory sociology with the same vigor and enthusiasm that we teach the upper-level courses in our specialties and do our research. We hope this book helps our colleagues who strive to contribute to this enthusiasm and respect for sociology.

Despite the fact that most students take only one course in sociology and most of these courses are *service courses* to the general education curriculum or other programs, many of these first courses also function as an "introduction to the major" course. So rather than providing students with relevant and useful information and perspectives for better understanding their experiences in society, the course often presents an encyclopedic collection of concepts and terms that give the impression that sociology is a discipline of disconnected jargon that is perceived either as "common sense" or as irrelevant to students' lives.

It is common practice in introductory sociology to adopt cafeteria-style textbooks in our courses that almost of necessity provide superficial overviews of central topics and specialties in sociology (Ballantine 1988). As good as many of these texts are, it is not difficult to see why Dave Barry makes fun of sociology. True, we occasionally recruit a new major or two in these introductory courses, but in reality, the vast majority, as many as 90 percent, of introductory students will never become majors in sociology or take another sociology course (Eberts et al. 1991).

Introductory sociology instructors need to recognize that they are not communicating as a solo voice in the presentation of the discipline. It is probably not in students' best interests to make the introductory course the place to present a single, favored theory or to suggest to students that other sociologists with different views are incorrect or misguided. Yes, we want to teach our students to think critically about theories and research, but we want students to see all the various perspectives within sociology. We argue that it is in students' best interests that presentations of research and theory in introductory sociology need to be balanced overviews and/or critiques of the discipline at this introductory level. Our challenge as teachers is to articulate the benefits of sociology, promote the goals of a general education curriculum, introduce the discipline of sociology, and most importantly, shape the abilities of our students to think critically and sociologically.

The Challenges of First Contact

A common assumption of instructors who teach the introductory sociology course (and there are many exceptions to this) is that this course is the introduction to our discipline and therefore we must *cover* everything that students might need as background and breadth in the discipline. This course is often the only prerequisite for other upper-level sociology courses, and we want our students to be well prepared. As a result, and perhaps too often, the introductory course superficially covers a little of everything, provides little in-depth material, and may or may not include a focus on the development of students' skills or thinking. The pressure to increase enrollments in our classes, of course, creates other challenges as well. There is no quick answer to the question, "What should be included in this course?" We will examine the issue of coverage in introductory sociology and evaluate its importance for this course.

We also observe that many introductory sociology courses today are textbook driven. Some instructors try to use *all* twenty-five chapters of an introductory sociology textbook. Others choose to cover fewer chapters in greater detail, assigning only eight to twelve chapters. This, of course, leads to the dilemma of which chapters to omit and which to include. Aren't they all important? Thus another aim of this book is to further discussion about the issue of coverage versus depth and/or skills. We also hope to provide the instructor of introductory sociology empirically based resources that will help plan a thoughtful, objective-driven course that presents sociology as a useful perspective and body of knowledge for our students. We will argue that mission, program, and course goals should drive the organization of a course and its readings, not the textbook chosen beforehand. We believe this is putting the cart before the horse.

The good news is that there are many sociologists who are wonderful teachers and many who are also talented and productive teacher-scholars. The literature in the scholarship of teaching and learning in both higher education and sociology has blossomed, and there is a plethora of literature about teaching and learning in sociology. Over the years, we have personally attended numerous sessions at meetings (many of them sponsored by the American Sociological Association's Section on Teaching and Learning in Sociology) and read many articles written by a cadre of very dedicated scholars in sociology who care immensely about teaching and learning. We can *and* should use these findings to help answer our questions about teaching and learning in the introductory sociology course. While there is still much research to be done, the wheel doesn't have to be reinvented. We hope to introduce or further familiarize instructors with the resources that are available from these colleagues and we offer some checklists which can be adapted and used in order to do this work more efficiently.

As ambassadors for our discipline, it is not enough to share vocabulary, concepts, theories, and research findings with our students and expect that they will go away with the ability to apply what they have learned to their lives or even find meaning in any of it. As instructors we can present the "worldview" of sociology by sharing our own stories and experiences. We can provide opportunities for students to write about their own experiences using their newly found sociological worldviews and encourage them to share these views orally in class. Using discussions as opportunities for students to frame their experiences in sociological terms is paramount for students to be able to use what they have learned after they leave the course. Sociology instructors have a tremendous opportunity to impact how the world sees our discipline, how students see the world, and whether and to what extent students will use sociology in their lives. Introductory sociology is our golden opportunity to share with students what we have to offer as a discipline and ultimately what our discipline has to offer the academic community as well as the wider social community. If we miss this chance or stumble through it, we have contributed to the public relations crisis in sociology and to lost opportunities to serve our students well. We need to make the most of students' *first contact*. It may be our only chance.

CHAPTER TWO

Discovering Your Students: What Does the Research Say?

Rationale for Finding Out about Your Students

Writers, speech makers, public relations specialists, and journalists alike have long known that one must *know one's audience* in order to communicate well to them. Not surprisingly, this is also very good advice for sociology faculty. Before we make that *first contact* with our students it serves both them and us as well to know something about them. How else can we set course goals and objectives, measure these objectives, or even begin to know how to relate and interact with students in ways that facilitate learning? Over twenty-five years ago, Goldsmid and Wilson wrote about this issue in their now classic book on teaching sociology, *Passing on Sociology* (1980). They argue that it is necessary to build bridges between us, as instructors, and students' experiences in order to effectively promote student learning. Indeed, as sociologists with training in symbolic interaction, most of us realize the importance of *shared meanings* in good communication. Goldsmid and Wilson state,

> To know others' experiences entails effort, since the instructor is separated usually by age or generation, by sex, perhaps by race or ethnic background and often by class, by region, and most often by commitment to the field of inquiry. (Goldsmid and Wilson 1980: 56)

The need to communicate effectively should provide sufficient rationale for instructors to take the time to learn who their students are before entering the classroom and taking attendance that first day. McKeachie (1978, 1994), author of a classic book for the college teacher, *Teaching Tips*, has long argued that knowledge about our students will help us "personalize education" by understanding their aggregate characteristics. Svinicki and McKeachie (2010 13th edition) suggest that this is just as important today as in the past. They provide many ideas for getting to know your students on the first day of class so that you can "break the ice" and set the tone for free communication, but also so that students and teacher will have better information about each other to aid learning. (We return to the topic of "breaking the ice" on the first day in chapter 8.) While it may be more difficult in a larger introductory sociology class than a smaller one to give each student the individualized instruction that might be optimal for learning, nonetheless by understanding aggregate student characteristics such as learning styles, motivations, demographics, psychological traits, and values we can better adjust the context and teaching styles to the diversity of our student populations, and we can find out some of this before the first day. Students at highly selective private universities no doubt have different aggregate characteristics than students at major public universities. These characteristics might very well overlap or diverge from the aggregate characteristics of students at four-year liberal arts colleges and universities or those at community colleges. What's a teacher who wants to connect with his or her students to do?

Anecdotally, a common error of some instructors, especially those who have come directly from graduate school, is the assumption that students at their undergraduate and graduate institutions will be essentially the same as those they meet in their first jobs. Indeed, if one could be a fly on the wall in any given faculty lounge, one might think that all students at all colleges or universities share much in common. Don't all students worry more about grades than learning? Don't they all wonder "if this will be on the test?" Don't they all think that faculty members conspire to set exams and due dates on the same dates just to make life more miserable for students? Were not the students of the past brighter, more hard-working, more courteous, and generally superior to today's students? Conversations overheard in many a faculty lunchroom might easily answer all of these questions, YES! All kidding aside, stereotypes abound about college students yesterday and today and probably tomorrow as well. But what can we do to learn who our students really are and what they really need? Let's look at some of the resources and research available for faculty.

Some Data about Students in General

In a 2004 issue of *The Chronicle of Higher Education* (itself a good resource for instructors for insights about students and other issues affecting higher education), Young describes a UCLA study of 276,449 first-year college students. Ninety-eight percent of these students graduated from high school in 2003, and 88 percent were A or B students in high school. Nearly 70 percent said they were attending their college of first choice and *only* 12 percent of them traveled 500 miles or more to attend college. Twenty percent had parents who did not attend college and only about 30 percent of their parents had a college degree (Young 2004). While this sample may not be generalizable to all first-year college students in the United States, as most were eighteen or nineteen years old, it does tell us something about the traditional-age college student.

This same study also tells us that about 10 percent of these students expect to major in social sciences and less than 1 percent expect to major in sociology. About 25 percent of students expect that they might need tutoring in math courses and about 10 percent might need tutoring in other non-math areas. But only a surprising 3.3 percent think they would need tutoring in their sociology courses. Hmm . . . since the vast majority of students only take the introductory sociology course, what does this tell us about student expectations in that first sociology course? How difficult do they expect it to be compared to their other courses? One interpretation of the above data suggests that students do not expect the introductory sociology course to be very difficult or challenging. What other expectations do first-year students have?

One study of community college students (Cravens 1996) had students in various introductory courses (sociology, psychology, business, chemistry, and biology) identify what they considered to be the top five instructor characteristics of excellence in teaching. While many students did not agree, the top five included the instructor's use of relevant examples, a clear emphasis on facts, the use of visual aids, the use of humor, and projecting enthusiasm. Moreover, students often identified opposite pairs as being important, such as both "flexibility" and "adherence to regulations." The second finding above (emphasis on facts) has implications for sociology instructors who have long argued that many first-year students have difficulty with disciplines such as sociology because they perceive it is often presented in ways that suggest there are no right answers or real facts. Helping students move away from the concrete thinking of their earlier academic lives to those of greater abstraction and theory can be a very challenging goal for any instructor. It is one we must confront in introductory sociology, however.

In other research, Feldman reviewed over thirty empirical studies and found that there was not perfect agreement between instructors' and students' expectations of effective college teaching. Students were more concerned that faculty were interesting, available, and helpful, as well as having good elocutionary skills (Feldman 1988). In this twenty-two-year-old review of literature, Feldman also found that students were more concerned about learning outcomes than were faculty. While emphasis on learning outcomes has substantially increased in the past two decades, it is interesting to note that students saw the importance of these *before* many faculty members did.

More recently, Filene summarized the research on student evaluations of teaching by noting that, in general, students value instructors who are enthusiastic, lucid, and organized as well as those who treat students fairly and caringly (Filene 2005: 107). The research on the topic has also demonstrated that students give higher ratings to courses which are intellectually challenging than they do to courses with light workloads (see for example Bain 1996). So while students and faculty may not be in perfect agreement about what constitutes effective teaching, there is a solid foundation on which we can build. George D. Kuh and colleagues (2005) argue that the key to successful learning and personal development is student engagement. The more time and effort students put into their studies the more likely they are to be successful. It's not exactly rocket science and it's no surprise to veteran faculty members. However, Kuh also argues that faculty members and institutions need to allocate resources, learning opportunities, and services to students in a manner that will induce students' participation in beneficial activities. This takes greater thought and preparation on the part of the instructor and drives home the point that we, along with our students, share responsibility for learning. We will address the topic of effective strategies for promoting student learning throughout the following chapters.

The U.S. Department of Education and their National Center for Educational Statistics provides useful statistics about college enrollments and student characteristics (Snyder et al. 2009). They report that enrollments (both graduate and undergraduate) have risen from 15.3 million students to 18.2 million students in 2007. Between 1997 and 2007 undergraduate enrollments alone have increased 26 percent (full-time students are up 34 percent and part-time students have risen 15 percent). Enrollments of women have increased 29 percent and males 22 percent. Younger, traditional-aged college students have increased by 16 percent during this same ten-year period. However, the proportion of students over the age of twenty-five has increased by 33 percent. These are trends which are expected to continue.

Students are a diverse population. For example, women continue to be the majority on most college campuses, and the number of traditional-aged college students is also increasing. These are national trends that many of us may see on our own campuses. But how can you check this out? Who are the students that *you* will meet in your classes? What can you learn before the first day of class?

How to Find Data about Your Students

Several resources and options are available for most teachers to use to learn about the social and educational characteristics of the students at their particular college or university. There are published volumes such as *Peterson's Guide to Undergraduate Colleges and Universities* or *U.S. News and World Report: America's Best Colleges*, where institutions make available information about their student populations. There are also many websites that provide access to similar information for prospective students and employees. These sources will tell you something about students' average SAT or ACT scores, the percent of students who are National Merit Scholars, and the number of applicants compared to the number admitted at each school. From such statistics one can surmise something about the selectivity of your campus. They also provide a view of your school that students encounter when they are "shopping" for colleges that most instructors may not share. But, the teacher should beware that these are statistics that are always presented to make the best possible impression of a school. Nonetheless it is a good comparative tool for finding out about student characteristics at your school.

Better yet, registrars and institutional researchers on your own campus can be valuable resources and provide a wealth of information about who your students are. Typically colleges and universities publish a campus or student profile annually that provides a demographic summary. If published information in the form of website pages (do look at your own college's website, if you haven't already) or brochures is unavailable, then contact these offices directly. The individuals who do this research vary from campus to campus, so don't be afraid to ask who does this task. The professional staff at your college or university can be very valuable colleagues and are generally very helpful with this task.

Perhaps the best, if not most direct way of finding out about your students, is *to ask them*. Many instructors hand out note cards or mini-questionnaires of one kind or another during the first class meeting. Students are asked to confidentially provide pertinent information about themselves including current cell phone numbers and e-mail addresses (which may be more current than what the registrar can provide faculty). But this is also an opportune moment to ask students to tell you other facts about who they are, such as their marital status, parental status, age, employment status, where they work, and how many hours per week they usually work. They can also indicate on this card their expectations for the course and whether they have special needs or health concerns that they would like to confidentially share with the instructor at this time. If instructors collect information in this way, they must, of course, guarantee to students that it is confidential and will not be shared with others. If teaching assistants will have access, students should be told this also. All information gathered must be voluntary. Students need to know that they are not required as a part of this course to provide any private information, but that doing so will aid the instructor to better know his or her students. Greenwood, co-author of this text, has been gathering such information about students for years and now finds that it is easy to see the patterns of student characteristics as well as the changes in them over the years. The one pitfall of this method is that you can't reasonably do this until the first class meeting . . . often too late to have the information for planning and syllabus construction. Nonetheless, it seems important to get this information in a concise and condensed format that can be referred to as needed. This information can be invaluable when students drop by your office, or you are meeting them to review for an exam, etc. It can be a springboard for conversation. It can help to better understand students' lives and time obligations. It also can be particularly helpful when a student misses an exam without notice, stops attending class, or just wants to talk with you. The instructor has a ready-made file of student information at his or her fingertips. Any tool that can facilitate conversation between teacher and student can become a bridge to getting to know one's students better.

Student Age Cohorts and Age Differences

If you teach at a university or college where the vast majority of students are of traditional ages, eighteen to twenty-four years, then you may only have an occasional student who is older. However, many universities and colleges today have more than a few nontraditional-age (which we will respectfully call "older" or "returning") students. In fact, some campuses have programs that target returning and older students and for yet others, returning and older students are the bread and butter of the campus population. Instructors, especially new instructors, need to be aware of and sensitive to the age diversity of students in their respective courses. Older students may have very different lifestyles and needs than younger ones. While some younger students have these characteristics, older adults are certainly more likely to have full-time jobs or careers, family and community responsibilities, and/or adult financial obligations. Older students are sometimes part-time and sometimes full-time students. Older students usually are paying for their own college expenses and often doing so at great personal and family sacrifice. While it is never ethically correct to treat one set of students differently from others, instructors need to be aware of older students' needs and responsibilities and respect them. As an example, an older employed student who is chronically late to class may have very different reasons for being late than a younger student. While both students' situations require respect and a private conference with the instructor to ensure that the class will no longer be disrupted, younger and older students may require different solutions to this problem. Indeed, all students may have legitimate reasons for missing class or turning in an assignment late. Our job is to recognize and be sensitive to such issues.

Research suggests that older students participate in class more often than younger students. This can be both a blessing and a problem in a mixed-age class. Research by Howard, James, and Taylor (2002) indicates that student age is an important predictor of class participation. They found that nontraditional students participated in class more often than traditional ones. Adult nontraditional students often bring to class a lifetime of real-world experiences, and they usually have developed clear attitudes about them that many are willing to share. They are also more likely to have experience with adult leadership roles. While this can enrich a class discussion, it might also intimidate younger students and inhibit them from participating as well. Instructors need to develop strategies for handling this situation so that discussion is not dominated by one or the other age group. For example, the instructor might make a class discussion policy so that students know that each student may contribute to the discussion no more than three times per session until everyone has participated. This can be an effective way of limiting those who might dominate, while providing opportunities for others who might be more reserved, regardless of age.

Cognitive psychologists and others who study human learning tell us that there are usually age-related changes in cognition, learning, and memory. While it would be difficult here to review all the relevant literature, it needs to be mentioned that while older students may have a larger, more complex cognitive framework (cognitive schema) within which they interpret, encode, and understand new information, younger students who might learn faster have smaller cognitive frameworks or schema. The latter may need to build frameworks, the former to alter existing ones. Moreover, it should be noted that gerontological research supports the notion that intellectual decline is not inevitable as we age (Schaie 1995). Other research suggests that most of us become more creative in some ways as we grow older (Simonton 1990). Those older students might just surprise you.

Research has supported, however, that older adults can take longer to learn new information than younger ones, but this may not necessarily always be due to age (e.g., it may be due to health issues, or because of new technology) (Poon 1995). These findings would be less true for twenty-five- to forty-year-olds as compared to students in their forties or older. Only about one-third of people demonstrate intellectual decline by their sixties (Schaie 1995).

Moreover, the older, returning student who has been out of school for a number of years may be disadvantaged by new or unfamiliar technology in the academy. It is hard for some young instructors to fathom a time in our not-so-distant past when library reference materials were not on computer databases, there was no Internet or e-mail, and where typewriters did the job of word processors. For the returning student, this new technology provides challenges with which they may need assistance.

Diversity in Social Characteristics

Increasingly, college campuses around the United States are more and more sensitive to racial and ethnic diversity issues (recent Supreme Court decisions about the extent to which race may be used in deciding college admission notwithstanding). As sociologists we are sensitive to the fact that people from different cultures, ethnic backgrounds, racial groups, and religious backgrounds bring to the classroom a range of rich experiences that are important in teaching and learning. Knowing who your students are also means understanding their cultural backgrounds and keeping them in mind as you plan your course and learning activities. For example, Jenkins discusses the need to understand cultural differences in what students perceive plagiarism to be, rather than jumping to the conclusion that these students do not understand what it is or are deliberately plagiarizing (Jenkins 2009). Jenkins looks at Native Indian cultures and evaluates the extent to which students find rewording or paraphrasing of experts' words as inappropriate, so they use the experts' words verbatim as a result of their cultural backgrounds. Recognizing these students' views of what is and what is not plagiarism will go a long way to helping educate them as to the rules in the academic culture about writing and citations.

Most sociologists agree that socioeconomic status is at least as important as race and ethnicity in determining one's life chances, if not more important. One way social class can impact the classroom is in the tenor of interactions. Middle- and upper-class students are likely to find heated, emotional exchanges in the classroom to be uncomfortable. They may interpret such behaviors as rude or even threatening. However, working-class students may feel interactions are deeper and richer when intense emotions are aroused. While middle-class norms dominate in higher education, we as instructors may have to actively work to help diverse students understand one another (hooks 1994).

Given the importance of social class, we need to know the social class backgrounds of our students as well. This might seem difficult to initially assess, but talk to your senior colleagues. They can provide valuable insight. Do some homework about the industry or business community in which your college is located. This is paramount on commuter campuses, but can be insightful on larger residential campuses as well where it is likely that at least some of your students will come from the local geographic area. One can ask on the student questionnaire distributed during the first session the occupations of parents of traditional-age students, but this would not be as useful for older, returning adults who confer their own social status rather than that of their parents. Other observations can also be beneficial. What kinds of cars do your students drive? What kinds of clothes do they wear? What other lifestyle variables give indications of social class standing? How many of your students are from families where they are the first to attend college? Answers to these questions may give insight into the class strata from which your students come.

So, are working-class students different from middle-class students or upper-middle-class students? Most assuredly yes in some ways and no in others. But let's talk about why this might be important to a teacher. Research by Szafran (1986) suggests that students with upper-middle-class and middle-class characteristics may arrive in introductory sociology already having greater sociological knowledge compared to lower-middle-class and working-class students. They may be better traveled and have visited other cultures as well. It is important for the instructor to know what students' socioeconomic backgrounds are in order to gauge what goals and course content might be most appropriate for this audience. Social psychological research also tells us that cognitive and linguistic styles may differ by social class. Lower-class and working-class students may arrive with different vocabularies and styles of language than their middle-class counterparts. This means that lower- and middle-class students may not have the vocabulary or articulation advantage of their upper- and upper-middle-class counterparts. It may also means that their expressions of language may not fit into the conventional upper-middle-class academic culture. Variations in class and culture here may create differences that are important to students' learning. This is another factor to consider in designing a course as well as preparing to make *first contact* with your students.

Needless to say, social class, ethnicity, age, or any other social characteristic should not be used to pigeonhole students into stereotypes. Aggregate data can and should be used to gauge averages, tendencies, or general characteristics of a population. Instructors are cautioned to always treat individual students with dignity and respect and recognize that they may not fit the pattern or the average case.

Students with Special Needs

In any given class of students, you are likely to encounter students with serious health problems, both emotional and physical, and students with disabilities (some more challenging for the student than others), as well as many students with social skill deficits.

There are federal laws (e.g., the Americans with Disabilities Act) governing access for disabled students, and there are usually staff on most campuses who are trained to ensure that your campus meets the needs of its disabled students. On larger campuses there may even be an office or center for providing such services. Nonetheless, faculty members have an obligation to provide equal access to learning for all their students including those with disabilities. This might mean making visual aids or exams available in larger type for the visually impaired student, allowing the audiotaping of lectures for the hearing-impaired, or allowing caregivers or note takers to be present in class and even during exams for the severely disabled student. It also means not overlooking the comments of the verbally challenged student who speaks more slowly or is more difficult to understand than classmates. It means making sure in confidential and dignified ways that each disabled student has what he or she needs to be a fully participating member of your class.

There are no federal laws governing how to best deal with emotionally impaired students who bring no formal medical documentation with them. Reece McGee (1991) in his book *Teaching the Mass Class* talks about a trichotomy of problem students: the psychotic, the illiterate, and the disorganized. These are not official terms, but McGee's many years teaching the large or mass introductory course led him to believe that students from each category will be present in any class. (See also Svinicki and McKeachie 2010.) McGee argues that students with such characteristics are proportional in every class regardless of class size. In the larger class, there is a greater likelihood that there will be more problem students and their issues to manage. McGee's guestimates are (based on his many years of teaching) that such students often require much more time and energy from the instructor in larger classes than smaller ones. While McGee was concerned about the larger absolute numbers of problem students with whom teachers of a mass class must contend, it is safe to say that all teachers must be prepared to deal with problem students. McGee describes the "personally disorganized" student as the individual who forgets assignments and test dates, whose backpack is a virtual whirlpool of papers and other disorganized items, both used and new. In a class of thirty-five students, McGee estimates that you might expect to have 8 percent, or two to three such students, but in a mass class there could be as many as forty in a class of 500. McGee suggests that "psychotic" students represent 2.5 percent of students in any class, and so in a typical class of thirty-five, maybe there is one student with special mental illness issues. In a larger class of 500, there could be as many as twelve or thirteen such students. What McGee calls "illiterate" students comprise about 12 percent of students on the average (in his experience), and a small class of thirty-five would likely have four or five students who lack appropriate reading or writing skills, and the mass class with 500 could have as many as sicty students. Indeed, these observations are based on Dr.

McGee's many years of teaching experience at a large, fairly selective land-grant university. It is entirely possible that on your campus you may have more or fewer such students in your courses. But to be sure, you will need diplomacy, tact, compassion, and other interpersonal skills to deal with such students in your classes. There is no simple rule or method for doing so, but it is important to be sensitive to students' problems in today's academic climate. At the same time, schools have developed different cultures about how to deal with problem students. Some types of problems are, of course, more intrusive on the classroom context or learning experience than others and, therefore, potentially bigger issues for the instructor. While classroom decorum is important, an underlying need may require directing the student to counseling or medical services and helping him or her follow through with those services. Students cannot be effective learners if their emotional health or personal problems are more pressing in their lives than their class work. While we are not trained as counselors, therapists, or personal coaches, as instructors we can point the way to such resources, educate students about getting help, and support them when they do so. This means that faculty members must be informed about the services and resources available to students on campus and in the local community. The first few years on a new campus this can be yet one more body of information for the instructor to learn, but it is an important one. Helping students to succeed can make the difference with regard to both retention and graduation rates at your college, but more importantly, it will make a difference in your students' lives.

Perhaps we could add the "uncivil" as a fourth category in McGee's typology. A commonly heard complaint among college teachers today is the growing extent of incivility of today's college population (see for example Benton 2007). Students seem to interrupt more often than in the past, students challenge professor's decisions more often, and, in general, they seem to be more confrontational. It also seems to be true that students often do not share the college professor's upper-middle-class rules of conversation or social conduct. In short, many experienced college teachers often find students today on the average to be rude and disrespectful compared to those of the past. Of course, we don't mean all students, but certainly there is a general trend in our culture that is mirrored in the academic microcosm and encountered by many instructors on a fairly regular basis. Ignoring the issue only contributes to the problem. How does an instructor appropriately respond?

For the mass class, McGee offers the solution of a behavioral contract with students which spells out both teacher and student expectations of conduct (McGee 1991). Students must sign and return the contract at the beginning of the semester. Of course, the most troubled students may need referral to a professional counselor or psychologist. This technique may be less appropriate in smaller colleges or classrooms. Other suggestions appear in the literature, but the one theme that is dominant, far and above the others, is to make one's expectations for behavior clear and do so within the cultural climate of your program. It is also important to think about this carefully and develop your own expectations about student behavior—ones that fit your teaching style, class climate, and course goals. It is also very important to communicate those expectations to students early, often, and clearly in various forms beginning with the course syllabus and/or policies that students receive in writing. It is important to do this with respect for the students as adults (even if some of them aren't yet), and it is necessary to communicate these expectations in a way that conveys that you care about them and about creating a favorable learning environment for them. These techniques help manage student conduct, but a chair and/or dean with a corroborative policy is also important in reinforcing this code when needed. It may help to talk with your colleagues and find out what the campus culture is about student conduct. Students (and even students' parents) today are more likely to complain up the chain of command than in the past. Don't be afraid to evoke the student conduct manual, handbook, or school policy if the college has one. Most importantly, keep the lines of communication open between you and your students. Be approachable, but firm, about what you expect and what the consequences will be if not followed. None of this will guarantee that you will not have problem students that make you want to go home and tear out your hair, students who think you are being grossly unfair because they didn't get an "A" on the test (and they always get A's), students who think you are out to get them or don't like them, and/or students who think they should be able to share their opinion at every juncture in class. There is no complete cure, but clarity and structure will help.

Sociology Majors, Minors, and Never-Again Students

One other typology of students is important in understanding *first contact* with today's introductory sociology students. Very few of our students come to us as sociology majors. A few will be "recruited" within the introductory course. These students will need an introductory course that will initiate them to their major. A few others will be sociology minors or in majors that require other sociology courses and will need a good foundation for further work in sociology, but perhaps not the same as the major. Yet others take the class because "it fit their schedule," "it sounded interesting," "they think they want to be a social worker," or "they want to learn about people" to understand or solve their own personal dilemmas. These are all legitimate reasons for enrolling. But most importantly, many students, if not the vast majority, whom we have *first contact* with will never again see the inside of a sociology classroom once they leave our introductory sociology course. Moreover, this typology is neither mutually exclusive nor exhaustive. For example, a student who takes our first course as a nursing major may end up two years later a sociology major. The challenge for the sociology instructor here, of course, is that each of these types of students expects a different course from the others and each type needs a somewhat different experience from the others. It is no wonder that it is difficult to satisfy all students in one first course.

Where this first course is embedded in the curriculum is paramount to meeting this challenge. Many introductory sociology, social problems, and social institutions courses are defined as general educational requirements for all arts, sciences, or university students. Thus the introductory course becomes a service to the general educational core of the college or university and will draw many more never-again types than a course that is a prerequisite only for upper-division work in sociology. In some universities this first course may meet a diversity requirement of the general educational curriculum as well, while for others the first course is the initiation into a disciplinary field of choice.

These are different curricular functions which can be at odds with each other. It is the challenge of the instructor (and the program) to determine how both sets of curricular goals can be met in one course.

In this chapter we have looked at the importance of knowing and understanding the students that you teach. We have provided some suggestions for finding out about them. And we have explored ways that students may have different needs depending on their age, ethnicity, race, social class, and/or disabilities. Finally, we looked at some types of problem students and how we might best provide them help. We conclude with the idea that it is the challenge of the scholarly teacher to find ways to meet the needs of all of these students. These challenges of course design and curricular context are addressed in the next chapter.

~

CHAPTER THREE

What Do You Want Your Students to Learn?

Course Content and Objectives

Planning to teach a new course can be a nerve-racking and agonizing experience. A lot of new material on teaching introductory sociology has been published in the past several decades. Even the experienced teacher may feel stressed about keeping current, updating a course, or making changes to what he or she has tried in the past. To make it a bit easier to find one's way through the myriad of ideas and imperatives in course planning, this chapter will provide an overview of important issues in course planning and content related to introductory sociology.

Placing the Course in a Context

An important initial issue that should concern most teachers, but is sometimes overlooked, is the awareness and consideration of the various contexts within which an introductory sociology course can be found. These contexts are sometimes obvious and at other times they may be implicit or even obtuse. They can be especially elusive to the person new to teaching, new to a campus, and/or new to a course. These contexts include institutional, program, and curricular contexts. Let's take Professor Jones as a hypothetical case. She is new, but a well-educated faculty member with great credentials and some teaching experience in graduate school and for two years in temporary, part-time positions that she held before landing a new tenure-track position here on our hypothetical campus. She has been assigned to teach introductory sociology among other upper-level courses in her specialty. She has taught this course before several times as a graduate student and once before in a temporary position. She knows the traditional content of introductory sociology as she learned it in her undergraduate and graduate training. She knows the kinds of textbooks that the course usually includes. She has also done her homework about what kinds of students she will likely see in her classes on this campus. But what doesn't Professor Jones know? Being new to the campus, Professor Jones will want to find out about her students as we discussed in the last chapter. But as a new person on campus she may not be completely familiar with the history and culture of her new campus. She probably doesn't know much about how the courses she will teach fit into a broader curricular and disciplinary context. She needs to ask some questions. Is there a long-standing pedagogical tradition at this school? Is the introductory course a *general educational* requirement or elective and for which students? Is the course expected to meet diversity or other specific curricular requirements in the general educational core? Is the course a *service* course primarily for non-majors? Is it the first course that students will take *in the major*? If so, should it then prepare students for work in other, future sociology courses? Are there core concepts that should be included in any first course in sociology? The answers to these questions will help Professor Jones begin to place her course in its various contexts and to know the central concepts that will help students understand and develop sociologically, but they will also help her to design the course that fits with institution and program objectives where she teaches. Designing an introductory course is a more complicated task than it first looks.

Programmatic or institutional contexts may dictate or influence course planning as well as how the course design can be executed. Some schools have a strong or long-standing tradition of using certain teaching styles or class sizes. Others, such as Alverno College, have adapted a very specific mode of teaching and learning based in assessment of student learning (Mentkowski et al. 2005). A good instructor needs to be aware of these contexts because they may provide insight for the emerging structure of a course, for the structure for student learning, and/or most likely for the overt or covert standards of evaluation by which the course will be judged successful. It is always helpful to talk with colleagues about these contexts. Instructors need to ask questions such as, what expectations do the department or schools have about this course? Another good place to begin is to read mission statements that the university, college, or program may have. These can provide useful information, but be sure to talk with colleagues about these mission statements rather than taking them verbatim. They could be old, outdated, or written for another audience.

Most, but not all, introductory sociology courses (and this might include the social problems course also) have a place in the larger college, school, or campus *general education* requirements. At different schools these may also sometimes be called G.E. or "gen ed" requirements, "core" requirements or courses, "breadth" requirements, "distribution" requirements, or freshman courses that all students are required to take. Sometimes students are given options of several courses from a list of core or general education requirements within which first-year sociology courses are offered. Often, sociology courses are included in a list of social science or humanities courses in general education options. The details will vary, sometimes significantly, from one college or university to another. Yet, there are many similarities in the general education curriculum and one of those similarities is the inclusion of first-year sociology courses. Not surprisingly, the rationale for sociology courses being included in general education is that sociology provides insight into society and/or perspectives that can benefit the student not only as college learner, but also as citizen, family member, and employee in today's world as well as in the world in which they will live in the future. Thus, first-year sociology courses in particular, and general educational requirements in the main, help broaden students' views and knowledge beyond that of their major. (See the reports published by the American Sociological Association, *Sociology and General Education*, 2005, and *Liberal Learning and the Sociology Major Updated: Meeting the Challenge of Teaching Sociology in the Twenty-First Century*, 2004, for a discussion of the role of sociology in general education and the goals of liberal education respectively.)

McGee suggests (among four other questions that we will look at later) that the first question we should ask should be, "What is the function of the course in the curriculum and what is its relation to other courses?" (McGee 1994: 345). At some colleges and universities faculty members have designed a specific course to meet general educational requirements. Smith (1990) describes one such sociology course that emphasizes the history of social and philosophical thought. This specific course arose from a desire "to integrate the introductory course with the goals and emphases of a synthetic, integrated core curriculum" (Smith 1990: 482). Roberts (1986) argues that introductory sociology instructors, in addition to thinking about content of their courses, need to consider the kinds of thinking skills the course should nurture in first-year students. Using a cognitive structuralist approach, Roberts suggests a number of goals and objectives for sociology courses in the general education curriculum. Both of these latter two studies are good examples of how faculty members have considered the broader curricular context and general educational needs in designing the first course in sociology. Yet, these are very different courses.

The challenge for teachers of introductory sociology courses is that often in addition to being part of the general educational curriculum, at the same time this course almost always serves as the introduction to the sociology major. Introductory Sociology is often a required course and prerequisite for taking other courses in sociology, especially upper-level courses for both majors and non-majors. Consistent with McGee's (1994) question above, we must also ask how this course fits into other course offerings in the major. Too often this leads to a couple of dilemmas. The first is that introductory sociology needs to provide all necessary prerequisites for all or any other sociology courses that a student may take, and the second is that it must provide all the basic fundamentals that students might need in order to continue course work in sociology. Whoa! This is asking a lot of just one course. Some colleges and universities have approached this dilemma by stretching out the course over a year or by providing one course for non-majors or transfer students and another for sociology majors. The latter option becomes more complicated when non-majors who have had the course for non-majors later change majors to sociology. It also raises the question: Does this mean that non-majors cannot take other upper-level sociology courses such as family, deviance, or stratification? Many schools, especially where sociology programs are small in size, earn their bread and butter by offering upper-level service courses to non-sociology majors. The large enrollments in courses open to non-majors as well as majors support the upper division offerings. This is a financial reality for many programs. For example, at one of the authors' universities the upper-level family course (with introductory sociology as a prerequisite) is taken by many other majors such as general studies, education, and nursing. We simply could not afford to stop offering this class to non-sociology majors and expect to have the enrollment numbers to support all the current faculty positions and course offerings that we currently have in our major. The small sociology program is supported by these types of offerings to non-sociology majors. Moreover, most sociologists would likely agree that it is both useful and important for allied majors to have opportunities to take sociology courses at both the lower- and upper-division levels.

In the original report published by the American Sociological Association and the Association of American Colleges, *Liberal Learning and the Sociology Major* (1991), introductory sociology as prerequisite for all other sociology courses is represented as a type of curricular structure using a "ferris wheel" analogy. Once you have taken introductory sociology, you have your ticket for any other sociology course. Apart from the problems this causes with course sequencing, developmental student learning, and other programmatic issues in the major (that are not the topic of discussion here), it *de facto* defines the introductory sociology course curriculum as well. This report suggests that introductory sociology must focus on key concepts within sociology, provide an overall view of sociology as a discipline, and provide opportunities for active learning of sociological skills such as empirical investigation or sociological thinking (Eberts et al. 1991). In the revised version of this report, *Liberal Learning and the Sociology Major Updated*, task force members suggest that we "get off the Ferris Wheel and develop a strong spine" (McKinney et al. 2004: 10) and that study-in-depth be promoted by offering a four-level sequence. The first level consists of sociology courses which do not have prerequisites. These courses usually are of general interest to students and often meet core or general education requirements, but are not foundational to other sociology courses. That is, we might want to design some first-level courses that are not conceived as "introductory sociology courses" that are expected to function as providing an overview of the discipline and preparing students for upper-level courses. These other, different, first-level or second-level (i.e. first- or second-year) courses would be designed to provide the skills and knowledge necessary to move on successfully in other advanced sociology courses. This model suggests that perhaps one course is not sufficient for the entry level of sociology. We might want to have a course or courses for general education purposes and another one for majors or collateral majors who want to do upper-level work in sociology. While this approach may not work in all college and university contexts, it is nonetheless an important issue to keep in mind when designing introductory sociology courses.

Becker and Rau (1992) argue critically that sociologists are not providing "good sound training in the discipline nor a really good sound introduction to the field for non-majors" (Becker and Rau 1992: 72). In their view this led to many of the problems which sociology faced for programs in the 1990s, including attracting intellectually less-competitive students, and programs being placed at greater risk of enrollment fluctuations. They suggest that sociology is too "specialty" ridden for its own good. The consequence of this for the introductory sociology instructor is that a good instructor needs to be well-versed in all the specialties of sociology, but also in related fields of interest to students *and* contemporary social issues as well. While this situation is not uncommon in other disciplinary fields, these authors suggest that the root of the problem is that faculty at a given school or program do not have shared expectations about what this course should entail. They further argue that sociologists as specialists often do not have shared understandings about what are central concepts in introductory sociology (Becker and Rau 1992: 74). We will return to the question of consensus about a core content in introductory sociology, but first let's examine the ways that issues of coverage can be handled in introductory sociology.

Three Models of Coverage

In thinking about content, at least three models of "coverage" in introductory sociology courses can be found. One model is the *cafeteria course* that provides a surface overview of the entire discipline, its concepts, theories, and methods. Many colleges and universities offer a course of this type and it is, perhaps, the kind of course about which Becker and Rau speak so critically. We have had many colleagues over the years who have told us that they cover all the twenty-five to twenty-eight chapters in a standard introductory sociology textbook in a one-semester course. Their argument is that all chapters are important to sociology and therefore should be included in the course. Some of these colleagues have actually been amazed at our own admissions of selecting only ten to twelve chapters to cover. Often our confessions are met with such exclamations as, "How can you leave out the chapter on demography and population?" "How can you *not* cover the chapter on (put your own favorite chapter title here)?" I have always found this question to be somewhat confusing. Book publishers feel compelled to include all those chapters, at least in part, because they want to sell their books to the widest possible market. If they leave out a chapter, it potentially cuts out part of that market and *ergo* their profits. In response to the above question, we usually state, "Just because a publisher has a chapter on a topic in a text, doesn't mean it is pedagogically significant to a particular course and its goals!" Typical responses to this statement range from "Oh!" to dead silence!

While there is nothing inherently wrong with the cafeteria model, it does pose problems of coverage. This reply to colleagues who use the cafeteria approach is couched in the fact that we use another model for introductory sociology courses. This second approach can be called a *fundamentals model.* Here the instructors select key chapters to cover in greater depth, leaving room for more discussion, active learning, collaborative learning, demonstrations, and/or visual media presentations. There clearly is a market here for such courses because many publishers offer textbooks which are "core" or "brief" editions of larger, more cafeteria-style texts. Moreover, it seems prudent to "cover" the basic theories and concepts of sociology that can be applied to our lives, and that will also be encountered in other courses as well.

A third approach can be called the *skills model,* where the content of the course is secondary to the objectives of learning critical and sociological thinking, problem solving, and/or the basics of scientific investigation. With less common core content than the first or second model, students individually or in teams study and investigate various topics related to the course. By comparison with the first and second models above, this approach to course design likely results in a course that covers substantially less content material than the traditional introductory sociology course, but ideally students come away with more-polished skills in writing, critical and sociological thinking, and/ or empirical investigation. This model is gaining in popularity with the growth of the "learning paradigm" (see discussion below) and a renewed emphasis at the national level on having students conduct research in all sociology courses. It can also fit well with the general educational goals of many institutions encouraging student research. Regardless of which model is used, an instructor might best serve his or her students and other publics by consciously thinking about which model of coverage they are adopting for the introductory course and how it will best serve the needs of the school, the course, and the students. This is the first goal of the instructor who designs and teaches introductory sociology.

Course Content, Student Learning, and the Learning Paradigm

Most instructors want to be or become great, or at least good, teachers. For many years the predominant way of thinking about pedagogy and teaching in general has been to concentrate on what teachers can do. Not surprisingly then, we evaluate good teaching on the basis of teacher behaviors rather than student behaviors or learning outcomes. Beginning in the late 1970s research in higher education in Sweden began to investigate *learning* rather than teaching (Biggs 1999). Swedish researchers were interested in the difference between *deep* learning and *surface* learning (Trigwell and Prosser 1991 in Biggs 1999), the latter being a less desirable outcome for students. It seems surprising that before this, in higher education, it was relatively unheard of to apply learning theories in psychology, social psychology, and sociology to help us better understand teaching and learning. Nonetheless, a paradigm shift began.

As these ideas took hold, some instructors in sociology began making changes. Atwater (1991) designed an introductory sociology course based on the ideas of a book by Katz and Henry, *Turning Pro-*

fessors into Teachers (1988), which placed the learner at the center of the course. These principles include (1) helping the student be active rather than passive, (2) recognizing the uniqueness of each student, (3) teaching the process and content of knowing, (4) helping students learn how to collaborate, (5) helping students learn to reflect, (6) recognizing the emotional aspects of learning, and (7) understanding the need for support in the learning process (of students and teachers) (Atwater 1991).

In 1995 an article by Robert Barr and John Tagg appeared in *Change* magazine. It caught the attention of many faculty and administrators in higher education. These authors contrasted the traditional paradigm in higher education (which they called the *instruction* paradigm) with a *learning* paradigm. They called for a rejection of the former by spurning the notion that teachers have responsibility for instructing. Rather, they argue, teachers and their colleges have the responsibility to *produce learning* (Barr and Tagg 1995: 15). Furthermore Barr and Tagg argue that students and instructors should be co-producers of learning and that students must take responsibility for their own learning. This is necessary at both the institutional level (e.g., looking at graduation and retention rates) but also at the individual level by devising and implementing high standards of learning. Further, they argue that "learning environments and activities are learner-centered and learner-controlled . . . and may even be teacherless" (Barr and Tagg 1995: 21). Under this paradigm, faculty roles include the designing environments for learners and providing students with the best tools for learning. The learning paradigm as defined by Barr and Tagg rocked the worldview of traditional academe. Teachers and students alike need to recognize their new roles. Learning, not teaching, is the center of our new universe.

Huba and Freed (2002) summarize this paradigm well in terms of eight hallmarks of learner-centered teaching. These hallmarks are (1) learners are involved and receive feedback, (2) learners apply knowledge to problems and issues, (3) learners integrate discipline-based skills and knowledge, (4) learners understand the character of excellent work, (5) learners become better learners, (6) professors coach and facilitate, (7) professors reveal they are learners, too, and (8) learning is interpersonal so all learners are respected and valued (Huba and Freed

2002: 53). Clearly the emphasis in this paradigm is on what's happening with the student and how the teacher can facilitate the student's learning. Again, they call for a reexamination of traditional "teaching" roles.

In a very nuts-and-bolts guide for the college teacher, Cannon and Newble place this discussion in the context of three kinds of behaviors to show that a learning objective has been achieved (2000). There are *knowledge* objectives, *skill* objectives, and *attitudinal* objectives. They argue that this typology of objectives parallels Bloom's (1956) famous taxonomy in the three behavioral domains, cognitive, psychomotor, and affective. Moreover, they argue that course content (for any course, not just sociology courses) should enhance intellectual development, must consider both ethical and moral aspects, and should contribute to deep learning (Cannon and Newble 2000). They also suggest that content should consider the professional criteria of the field, psychological criteria, practical criteria, and student criteria.

We can apply Cannon and Newble's three types of objectives by considering each category. *Knowledge* objectives might include factual information about theories as well as empirical research findings. *Skill* objectives include critical thinking, the use of empirical support in arguments, and research methodologies as examples. Finally *attitudinal* objectives may include greater understanding, appreciation, and tolerance of diversity, cultural relativism, and social values affecting students' lives. It might also include developing an attitude appreciative of the scientific method in sociology.

Weimer (2002) tells us that in the new learning paradigm we must reject teacher authoritarianism and even challenge faculty expertise in the classroom. The teacher needs to move from being the "sage on the stage," who always knows the "right" answer and is the fount of wisdom which is imparted to passive students, to the "guide on the side" who recognizes that he or she still has much to learn and engages in the learning process with students. In many ways, the learning paradigm is a freeing process for faculty members because students are charged with the responsibility for their own learning. Teachers guide, facilitate, discuss, and provide the tools needed for student learning as well as assess learning. But ultimately, students must accept that they must actively contribute to their own learning rather than being passively dependent upon the instructor to "teach" them. Weimer identifies the core of resistance to the learning paradigm or skills model. It is a cry often heard by faculty across campus. "How can I *cover* all the needed material if I take too much time for other activities?" She states, "Strong allegiance to content blocks the road to more learner-centered teaching" (Weimer 2002: 46).

So, here we are back to the same dilemma. How much and which material should be covered in an introductory course, and how much time should I spend providing opportunities for students to learn other important skills such as critical reading and thinking, writing, speaking, problem-solving, or interpersonal skills? Obviously there is no one correct answer to these questions. It depends on who your students are and what they need, the context of your course (to the institution or program), and one other important factor. What does your institution and/ or program want students to learn? What do you and your colleague faculty members want your students to learn in your course? All of this is predicated on the idea that we understand that these may not be individual decisions; nonetheless, you as the instructor must ultimately decide what goals and objectives you want students to achieve in this course and then think about realistic ways to assess that learning. Ideally this should be done in collaboration with your sociology colleagues. But let's look at some of the ideas sociologists have had about what core ideas are central to sociology and the introductory course.

Background on Core Content in Introductory Sociology

Our generation of sociologists is not the first to think about this issue of coverage versus skills. Not surprisingly, a number of sociologists have written about the content of sociology curriculum in general and the content of introductory sociology in particular. Beginning about thirty years ago, with the publishing of *Passing On Sociology: The Teaching of a Discipline*, Goldsmid and Wilson (1980) outlined some field-related goals for teaching sociology such as teaching basic social facts and data, basic concepts, major theories, and knowledge of "critical hypotheses and the results of empirical testing" (p. 65). However, they also devoted an entire chapter to discussion of goals that transcend sociological content, such as the methods of social inquiry and methods of extending knowledge to new situations; in short, "the processes of gaining and extending knowledge" (Goldsmid and Wilson 1980: 119).

A few years later, William D'Antonio, sociologist and a former Executive Officer of the American Sociological Association, wrote about "nibbling at the core" (1983). He shared his own frustration in trying to get his departmental colleagues to come together to find a common core curriculum in introductory sociology. His experience was not uncommon from those of many sociologists today. Several of his colleagues accused him of transgressing the inviolate rule of "academic freedom." His colleagues obviously felt that they should be able to teach whatever content within sociology they as individuals deemed appropriate. It is ironic that some sociologists, who readily recognize that knowledge is socially constructed, fight against any attempts to collectively define the scope of knowledge for the introductory course in the discipline, arguing that it should be a matter for individual instructors to define. While academic freedom is precious, it is not clear to us why designing a collaborative introductory sociology curriculum should threaten so many of us. It may well mean more work for us as instructors as we adapt our courses to the collectively agreed-upon curriculum. We might even be asked to teach something we have not included in our course in the past or something we didn't learn about in graduate school. But isn't that the same thing that we ask of our students in our classes—come and learn something new? In his article, D'Antonio (1983) outlined a core set of topics for the introductory sociology class and eloquently explains why each item needs to be included in the courses. His core is summarized below:

Theorists and Their Theories
1. Durkheim, Marx, Mead, Weber
2. Functionalism, Conflict, Symbolic Interaction
Sociological Concepts
1. Theoretical: the stuff of sociology, as embodied in the seminal writings of these theorists and developed by others, is found in:
   a. The human group, the social system, social organization
   b. Structured social inequality, including inequality by age, sex, race, and ethnicity, and the inequality of economic

and political systems, class, status, and power, and related concepts

c. Socialization, the social nature of self, role learning, and the place of the individual in the group

d. Social change, industrialization, urbanization, demographic transition, and bureaucracy

2. Methodological:

a. Social facts, concepts, generalizations, hypotheses, and theories

b. Variables (dependent, independent, and intervening)

c. Participant observation, questionnaires, and interview schedules, use of local records

d. Reading and constructing percentage tables

e. Sampling (D'Antonio 1983: 173)

An experienced introductory sociology instructor can make a quick review of this list of topics and realize that this is, indeed, a familiar outline adapted by most introductory textbooks today and, not surprisingly, it is used in many courses. Nonetheless, D'Antonio goes on to tell us that teaching sociology includes more than teaching the above topics. It should also be about teaching the ability to separate sociological facts from common sense, family beliefs, or other fictive ideas about the world. Once again coverage is not enough; one must also teach skills and provide opportunities to practice them.

Gerhard Lenski (1985) wrote an article on the introductory course where he criticized the common content found. Lenski argues that introductory sociology courses need to consider macro, mezzo, and microsociological domains. But most importantly, he wanted introductory sociology to have a strong historical/comparative content. Lenski made this perspective the focus of his model for the introductory sociology course.

Davis (1985) tells us that demonstrable empirical regularities could be the organizing principle of introductory sociology. He suggests that those empirical results which are (1) very true, (2) easily demonstrable, (3) about causal systems, (4) sociological in perspective, and (5) thought-provoking should be the goods that we share with our students while at the same time teaching the empirical scientific basis of sociology (Davis 1985: 154–55). Davis provides five clearly teachable examples using data from the National Opinion Research Center (NORC) that can be taught in introductory sociology. While his theme includes concepts such as cohorts, educational attainment, homogamy and privilege, as well as attitudes, Davis's model could be updated and applied to other substantive areas.

In an article called "The Essential Wisdom of Sociology" written by well-known methodology textbook author Earl Babbie, the author initiates a springboard for discussion about content in sociology by presenting ten basic principles that might be included in introductory sociology. These are summarized here:

1. Society has a *sui generis* existence and reality.
2. It is possible to study society scientifically.
3. Autopoiesis: Society creates itself.
4. Cultures differ widely across time and space.
5. The individual and the society are inseparable.
6. Systems have system needs.
7. Institutions are inherently conservative.
8. Explanatory sociology is implicitly deterministic.
9. Paradigms shape what we see and how we understand.
10. Society is an idea whose time has come. (Babbie 1990: 526–29)

This article generated responses from numerous other sociologists to which Babbie responded favorably that he should add at least two more principles:

11. Social life is dynamic.
12. Sociologists practice empirical research (perhaps a corollary of #2 above). (Babbie 1990: 540)

Although Babbie was criticized for an apparent structural-functional bias, we still find his twelve items helpful in our discussion. Nonetheless, this piece did exactly what it was supposed to. It generated discussion about these important topics. This is a goal of this book as well.

In 1991 an article by Wagenaar in *Teaching Sociology* proposed goals for the discipline of sociology. While these goals were directed toward the sociology major rather than one particular course in sociology, they provided a starting point for discussion of content in sociology courses. The article later became published as a part of the ACC's *Liberal Learning and the Sociology Major* (Eberts et al. 1991) and was a pivotal point for change in sociology curriculum using the learning paradigm and a new focus on student learning and assessment. It was adopted or adapted to many sociology programs around the United States. The updated version of this document should be required reading for all sociologists who teach, design, and assess sociology curricula. A new version of the document titled *Liberal Learning and the Sociology Major Updated* was released by the American Sociological Association in 2004.

The article by McGee (1994) mentioned earlier discusses the content of introductory sociology. McGee provides five questions to help guide course planning. The first one we have already discussed: (1) "What is the function of the course in the curriculum and what is its relation to other courses?" (1994: 345). We have already discussed the second question in chapter 2: "What is the nature of the course's audience?" (1994: 345). Question 3 asks the instructor to be cognizant of the school calendar: "How many class days are there in the term?" (1994: 346). This question asks us to attend to very practical time constraints. The fourth question asks, "How much writing will or must you require in the course and for what purpose? (1994: 346). Here McGee is asking us to consciously think about opportunities students will have to demonstrate learning, but also to practice the application of sociological concepts and sociological thinking. Finally he asks us to think about how course content influences assessment with the question, "What kinds of evaluation procedures do you propose to use and how will you use them?" (1994: 347). This final question is a topic that emerges from course goals and objectives and one to which we will return in another chapter.

Is There a Core for Introductory Sociology?

Research about a "core" in sociology continues. Wagenaar (2004a, 2004b) writes about the results of a survey with an availability sample of 301 sociology instructors who were asked about this issue. With regard to the introductory sociology course there was some agreement among instructors about the inclusion of a few concepts (Wagenaar 2004b). Instructors tended to rank highest on their list concepts such as "sociological imagination," "differences, inequality, and stratification," and "individual and society." Interestingly, "applied sociology" and "methods and statistics" ranked lowest (Wagenaar 2004a). Wagenaar states,

> Overall, the results show that the highest rated core items for the introductory course include several basic concepts—sociological imagination, social structure, culture, and socialization—as well as several items pertaining to differences and inequality. Two skills are also included: sociological critical thinking and thinking like a sociologist. (Wagenaar 2004a: 10)

If these findings are generalizable to all instructors in sociology, then we can conclude that sociologists have at least *some* agreement about what should be "covered" in the introductory course. Only the two skills mentioned above are consensually important for this first course.

Introductory sociology as it is taught today is more concerned with *coverage of topics* than students learning skills other than critical and sociological thinking. Moreover, Wagenaar found that values and commitments as a part of the introductory course are ranked the lowest and that skills were ranked higher for the larger sociological curriculum than for the introductory course. He suggests that introductory sociology may not be well linked to broader general educational goals such as critical thinking, effective writing, and so on (Wagenaar 2004a).

Wagenaar's (2004a, 2004b) research about core concepts in sociology led to published conversations about the core in sociology in *Teaching Sociology*. Keith and Ender (2004b) argue that less than 10 percent of sociologists in Wagenaar's study agreed "that any one of these concepts or outcomes ought to be placed among the top five priorities" (Keith and Ender 2004b: 39). They observed that at least 90 percent of the sociologists in this study have differing ideas about the core concepts in studying sociology. Keith and Ender conclude that there seems to be some skepticism among sociologists about the extent to which there actually is a consensual core as opposed to hoping there is one (2004b: 39).

In a different article in this same issue of *Teaching Sociology*, Keith and Ender (2004a) examined textbooks in introductory sociology looking for evidence of a consensual core across books. They looked at books published in two different decades: the 1940s and the 1990s.

They argue that if a core exists there should be evidence of greater consensus in texts published in the 1990s as compared to the 1940s and less variability of concepts within decades. Indeed, they found a greater reliance on concepts in the 1990s than in the 1940s. They also found some agreement that eleven concepts were part of the core, including the following: caste, culture, ethnocentrism, family, folkways, group, institutions, religion, society, and sociology (Keith and Ender 2004a). However, they also found that 50 percent of concepts appear only once among textbooks and fewer than 3 percent of concepts can be found in 90 percent of all the books (Keith and Ender 2004b). Moreover, the number of solitary concepts (concepts used by only one book) did not decline between the two decades. Perhaps we have less core in sociology that many of us believe we do.

Persell and her colleagues conducted research surveying peer-recognized leaders in the field of sociology (ASA presidents, award recipients, grant recipients, etc.) and presented more optimistic findings. They found nine major themes that most of their respondents agreed should be found in introductory sociology (Persell, Pfeiffer, and Syed 2007). These nine themes include the following:

1. The "social" part of sociology, or learning to think sociologically
2. The scientific nature of sociology
3. Complex and critical thinking
4. The centrality of inequality
5. A sense of sociology as a field
6. The social construction of ideas
7. The difference between sociology and other social sciences
8. The importance of trying to improve the world
9. The importance of social institutions in society

If the leaders selected for this study are good spokespersons for our discipline, then we can see that there may be more agreement about what should be taught in the introductory sociology course than prior research suggested. Differences in findings may also be a result of sampling differences. Persell et al. (2007) surveyed "leaders in the field" as compared to Wagenaar's (2004) availability sample of sociologists. One could make arguments for either sample representing the discipline better than the other. Neither was a random sample per se. Of course, each study asked different questions and measured consensus differently. But we conclude that this is a question that our discipline should be addressing and we, as instructors, should be thinking about and talking with our peers about as we design curriculum and courses.

Of course, there may be other concepts, theories, and/or skills which may need to be included in your course as consequence of the idiosyncratic characteristics of your students, your institution, and/or your curricular goals, but the authors of this book agree that these nine themes can be a starting point for developing the core elements of a good course.

In a 2007 *Teaching Sociology* article, Howard and Zoeller examined students' perceptions of gains in general education goals as a result of participation in an introductory sociology course at a large midwestern public university and its smaller extension campus. They found that students reported the greatest gains on "integration and application of knowledge," "critical thinking," and "understanding of society and culture." Thus one could argue that the development of abilities or skills is an outcome of introductory sociology and should be more intentionally cultivated by sociology instructors.

Putting It All Together

The most important conclusions that we hope will be drawn from the discussion about course planning and the content of introductory sociology include the following:

(1) Curriculum and course planning and construction should be a reflective, thoughtful, consensual, and explicit process. We should consider our audiences as well as the various contexts within which we offer our courses.

(2) Instructors need to identify and make explicit several specific course goals that can later be observed and measured for their outcomes.

(3) Course content needs to include key concepts that are central to the discipline of sociology such as social structure, culture, socialization, and inequality, but need not be inclusive of all areas of specialty within sociology. Ideally, faculty who teach the introductory course should have discussions with their colleagues to develop a consensus in coverage needed within a given program.

(4) Finally, and equally important, instructors need to facilitate learning beyond coverage of content and provide students with opportunities to learn and practice skills such as "developing a sociological imagination" or critical thinking.

In the next two chapters we consider both the syllabus and textbook as aids to student learning and elements of the introductory sociology course. First we turn to the textbook.

CHAPTER FOUR

∼

Tools of the Trade—
The Textbook

Students in introductory sociology courses often have *first contact* with the textbook and syllabus used in introductory sociology before anything else. In the advent of online-assisted courses, increasingly many students "meet" these elements of their class *before* they meet the instructor. As such, they become important in setting the tone and expectations for a course and are paramount in importance as elements in a teacher's toolkit. Their content can help or hinder student learning. In this chapter we address issues related to textbooks. A discussion of syllabi will follow in chapter 5.

Assigned readings can either reinforce course objectives or make teaching and learning more difficult. Readings can spur students to read more, to ask questions that facilitate learning, to think critically. Alternatively, poorly chosen textbooks or readings can confuse students with poor organization or examples which are outdated or irrelevant to students, and leave students sleeping on their books. Anecdotally, some students report that they do not buy or read the book at all but rely solely on lectures and classroom notes. It is also noteworthy that in the past few years, the amount of published articles about textbooks in sociology has diminished. Perhaps it is time to address some of these issues again. We examine the use of textbooks and other reading alternatives, how they can enhance or hinder teaching and learning in the introductory course in sociology, and some issues related to the quality and diversity of texts available today.

Textbooks, Textbooks, and More Textbooks

A new teacher can be easily overwhelmed by the number of books available for use in the introductory sociology course. Moreover, they may appear to be "clones" of each other while at the same time have important differences. In the first part of this chapter we will provide an overview discussion about the textbooks available for introductory sociology, where to find them, and their organization, content, and functions for this course. We will present the arguments pro and con for using textbooks in introductory sociology as well as choosing the alternatives. Finally, we provide criteria for selecting a text for your course.

Let us also begin by saying there is no single "right" answer when it comes to textbook choice. In fact, we take very different approaches with Greenwood favoring more traditional survey textbooks and Howard rejecting survey texts altogether in favor of readers. What is important is finding books which support *achievement of course goals and objectives*, which are *appropriate for your students and your context*, *complement or supplement your classroom activities*, and work with your *style of teaching*.

An instructor has a number of options available for textbook selection today. At least three types of books for use in introductory sociology are available: the "big book" which aims to provide a comprehensive survey of the discipline, the "core" text which also surveys the discipline but more briefly, and the reader or anthology of selected readings which address key topics in introductory sociology but typically do not intend to provide a survey of the discipline but rather provide access to primary resources, empirical articles, or journalistic accounts of social issues. We'll discuss each in turn.

The "big book," as it is often called, is the cafeteria-style text. It is usually a hard-bound text with as many as twenty-five or thirty chapters and usually the most expensive of the options we discuss. "Big books" include many features that purportedly aid learning such as vocabulary lists, glossaries, lengthy chapter summaries, boxed inserts of related material, links to pertinent student and faculty websites, and suggestions for further reading. They are usually expected to *cover* (there's that word again) just about every conceivable topic, theory, or issue in contemporary sociology and thus are very encyclopedic in nature. While they are often written by one or more sociologists, it is not uncommon for them to be what McGee (1985) called author-assisted (i.e., written by a ghost author or editor who is not a sociologist and is often a professional textbook writer). Taking this trend to an extreme are books that are called "managed texts." These are usually written without the primary authorship of sociologists and are written by writers employed by the publisher or other professional writers. McGee dislikes managed texts because they are creations for the market and may have less concern with intellectual criteria valued by faculty. Moreover, he charges, they sometimes use as sources other textbooks rather than monographs and research articles. They cater to "hot topics" in the media and popular social positions rather than objective overviews of topics or issues (McGee 1985). While the appearance of managed books seems to have diminished since the mid-1980s, they are still among us. There are examples of such books available for introductory sociology. Some texts written in the 1980s were purportedly good examples of the managed text—one that was not necessarily written by a sociologist but rather a professional textbook writer. It is always a good idea to check the academic credentials of the books we adopt. Author-assisted books appear to have emerged from the dislike of managed texts (McGee 1985). These texts have sociologists as authors where publishing houses provide various kinds and levels of assistance to the authors. At times they may look as if they are sole-authored by sociologists and at other times they may appear more like a managed text. This is a very common way that "big books" are written today, if only because it is a daunting task to *cover* everything in the discipline in one book. The market demands of textbook publishing are very powerful forces shaping textbooks.

Faculty members are able to influence the quality of textbooks when asked to review chapters of new or revised manuscripts and when they are asked to answer surveys about their courses and textbook needs. But beware! Often these reviews and surveys are merely marketing tools to familiarize the instructor with the text in hopes that an adoption will ensue. Kendall (1999) explains this review process and its pitfalls and distinguishes between *content* reviews and *marketing* reviews. The former are part of the writing and editorial process and reviewers can have a real effect on the final version of a text. The latter are, as mentioned above, the publisher's attempt to find their niche in the market and sort out potential adopters. They are usually conducted much later in the writing process (often the book is already in production). Marketing reviews have less impact on the content of the material in the textbook.

But why are we spending so much time and ink here explaining this process to you, the instructor of introductory sociology? Ultimately, faculty members are the adopting audience of textbooks. They, alone, or with a team of colleagues and perhaps a few students, decide which book will be adopted and sold in the campus bookstore and which ones students will buy online. We estimate that 75 to 90 percent of introductory students use textbooks. This could include as many as 700,000 students a year. Publishers are scrambling for a share of this market. Choosing to adopt or not adopt a textbook is the most important way that faculty influence the quality of textbooks available today. Books that are not adopted, that do not sell, are not reprinted or revised and do not remain available very long. Of course, you can write your own textbook. But this is a huge task that is better suited for a discussion in yet another book . . . or at least for later in this chapter.

Big books can be divided into at least two categories: *theoretically eclectic* and *theoretically focused*. The largest proportion of these is the *theoretically eclectic* book. It has been a trend for the past couple of decades for many books to try to offer a balanced theoretical perspective. They offer overviews and applications of major theories in sociology including structural-functionalism, conflict theory, symbolic interaction, exchange theory, and feminism. While many of these textbooks provide only introductory overviews of each theory in the first chapter or two, some texts do a better job of integrating the application of theory throughout the text. The best books provide opportunities for students to think critically about these theoretical perspectives and begin to use them. The eclectic book is very popular today. Two examples of some of the best-selling eclectic books include those written by Schaefer (2010) and Macionis (2010) but there are many others as well. Over half of the books available are eclectic. Moreover, if it is a program or course goal of your class to introduce major theoretical perspectives, then this kind of book might serve your students well. Critics have argued, however, that no book can really give fair presentation to all the theories in a page or two of a chapter (Graham 1988). We argue that the best texts (with regard to theory) integrate these theories throughout the text rather than in just one chapter, thus showing students how theories can be used and applied to a variety of social issues and problems.

The *theoretically focused book*, as the name suggests, uses one or perhaps two theoretical perspectives consistently throughout the book. Examples of this approach include Eitzen, Baca Zinn, and Smith (2010) written from a conflict perspective and Henslin (2008) which places greatest emphasis on an interactionist approach. Another very good example of this approach is the Nolan and Lenski (2008) text, which has been around for many years. It thoroughly and consistently presents a social historical/comparative perspective on sociology. Lenski (1985) argues that most courses leave out this perspective that he deems central to sociology. He designs his entire introductory course around this theme. The textbook written by Nolan and Lenski reflects instructor course goals and suits such learning outcomes well. While there is certainly room in sociological pedagogy for theoretically focused introductory courses and places where this kind of course would best fit the programmatic goals of a department or college, these books would not meet the needs of many programs or courses with eclectic course goals. One has to also ask how well students will be prepared in other sociology courses they may later take, if they have not had a more broad exposure to theoretical perspectives in the field. The textbook chosen here could be very important to student learning in the introductory course as well as in the future.

Another variation of the "big book" can be described as *Core* textbooks. They are often written by the same authors who write the "big books." After completing a successful big introductory book, publishers often ask authors to write brief or condensed versions of their books. These "core" texts are usually paperback texts and have a slightly reduced cost to students. They leave out the "frills" and have boiled down discussions of concepts and issues. They usually have fewer chapters than the "big books." Nonetheless, they are very popular with faculty who are concerned about textbook costs for students, faculty who might want students to purchase other books for the course, and those whose courses focus on coverage of fundamental concepts in sociology rather than surveying the entire field. Another strength of core texts, in addition to price, is that the condensed approach results in a book that reads a bit less like an encyclopedia or dictionary of sociological terminology. Being less lengthy, this type of text may also help instructors who struggle with the coverage issue. While not recommended, if one is going to try to cover all or most of the chapters in the book, it helps if the chapters are shorter and more focused.

A somewhat new variant on the brief or condensed book are texts that model commercial magazines. They are full of colorful graphics and lots of visual attention-getting devices with brief narratives covering the material. One recent example is Carl's (2011) *Think Sociology*. The cover of the book looks very similar to any contemporary magazine at the newsstand, with a well-tattooed, female model as the centerpiece and short phrases and sentences enticing the reader to go to certain pages for answers. It is clear that these books may be more inviting to younger readers but the trade-off may be the presentation of sociology as a less-than-scholarly discipline.

A third approach to introductory sociology course books includes the *reader* or anthology of collected articles, usually edited by one or more sociologists. They are varied in content but can include "classic," primary articles by sociology's great authors (e.g., Karl Marx, Max Weber, Charles Horton Cooley, George Mead, Lewis Coser, C. W. Mills) or they may include articles taken from contemporary sociological journals of a theoretical or empirical nature. Other readers are collections of "lay" articles from newspapers, magazines, and other non-sociological publications (e.g., *Annual Editions*). Yet others incorporate selections from all of these categories. They can be used to supplement a standard textbook or they can be used alone. As a supplement to a text, readers can offer students the opportunity to read, discuss, critically analyze, write, or speak about primary sources. Such readings may help students see the scholarship behind the textbook. But used in conjunction with a textbook, it not only adds to the amount of reading students are asked to complete and understand, it also increases their textbook costs.

Using a reader or anthology as a stand-alone text in an introductory course has its challenges. In fact, the strengths of using readers are also the challenges of doing so. While the articles in readers provide students an opportunity to grapple with primary sources, they are not usually written by authors with undergraduate students in mind. These articles were most likely not written as teaching tools. The variability of writing styles, vocabulary, and readability may vary greatly from article to article. Depending on the abilities of your students, these books might require more review in class and assistance from the instructor to assure that students comprehend important issues. At the same time, providing students the opportunity to learn how to read and master primary sources and how to grapple with a variety of writing styles can be a valuable building block for courses which come later in the curriculum as well as provide opportunities for critical thinking.

On the other hand, many readers do not tie together well the articles using prefaces or extensive summary articles. Summaries written by the editor may justify inclusion or demonstrate exactly how all the articles are organizationally connected. Without these bridges, students can lose the "big picture." Having used these anthologies in many courses in the past, we suspect that many students do not read the introductory articles written by the editors. (To be fair, the encyclopedic/dictionary approach of many big book and core texts may discourage students from reading them as well.) Selection of a reader as a stand-alone text or as a supplement to another text requires careful consideration of who your students are, their reading abilities, their monetary resources, and their time commitments. It also requires the instructor to be prepared to provide the potentially missing framework for the course perhaps through lecture, class activities, or in web-based support materials. Yet, if the value the instructor adds to the course is merely recapping and explaining what is covered in the "big book" or "core" textbook, they may not be necessary to achieve course goals and objectives. Instructors need to ask themselves, what do the textbooks add to a course that I as the instructor am not already providing? Given the high cost of most survey textbooks, if the big book or core text is not adding significant value, a more engaging reader may be an appropriate alternative text for the course. At the same time, using a reader may mean that students will need to rely on class lecture, discussion, and activities to provide the organizational framework for the course that a reader may not provide. For the new instructor, or one just out of graduate school, this places a great deal of responsibility squarely on his/her shoulders for providing the expertise needed to meet eclectic course goals.

Another option for instructors to consider when looking for introductory sociology readings is the trade book. Such books are usually short pieces emphasizing a few important concepts in studying sociology for the first time such as the sociological imagination, inequality, and/or socialization, and they can be used to complement any reading list. Examples of such books written expressly for the introductory sociology market include but are not limited to Richard Schaefer's *Sociology Matters* (2011), Joel Charon's *Ten Questions* (2009), and Charles Lemert's *Social Things* (2008). Such books can be used alone, with a standard textbook, or with an edited reader. Of course, almost any trade book on a sociological subject can also be adopted by an instructor in the introductory course. However, because they are not necessarily written as textbooks, one needs to be certain that they are readable for the first-year student at the campus where the course is taught. It is also possible, of course, to use books written by non-sociologist authors. We have even seen instructors adopt fictional books in successful ways. However, fiction or nonfiction books written by non-sociologists raise issues related to demonstrating to students the theories and methods of sociology. Since these trade books are not textbooks per se, it becomes difficult to evaluate their use in any standardized way. The most important criteria that should be used when considering trade books for adoption is the extent to which these readings will assist student learning (i.e., that they will help meet the learning objectives for the course). It also seems important to us to consider the book's sociological approach to the topics or issues discussed. It is possible to provide this for students in class or online if it is missing from the readings; however, this could be a risky venture depending on the instructor's experience as well as the abilities of the students in the course. As ambassadors to our discipline, it seems worthwhile that we at least consider selecting books and articles written by sociologists.

Over the years, we have heard complaints from students when a second book is required for a course and then not fully read or used in the course and/or when secondary reading materials (i.e., readers) become repetitious in content with the primary text. Students may feel that their monetary resources are being misused or exploited, especially when they have to purchase hundreds of dollars worth of books each semester. It is a serious mistake to require students to purchase a book and then not require them to read substantial portions of it. It is a sure-fire way to upset students! Books which are offered in e-book format can be less expensive for students. We suspect that this is the wave of the future.

There is also the issue of which textbooks our students will actually bother to read. Howard (2004) conducted an eight-semester study of students in his introductory sociology classes. Based on student end-of-semester self-reports, he discovered that only 40 percent of all students reported that they "usually" or "always" read the assigned pages in the "Core" textbook. Only 30 percent of students who learned lower grades (C, D, or F) in the course reported "usually" or "always" reading the core textbook. Only slightly more than half the A and B students reported reading the core textbook. In comparison, almost 70 percent of students reported "usually" or "always" reading assigned pages in one reader and over 93 percent reported they read assigned pages in a second reader. In conversations with students and through comments in student course evaluations, Howard concluded that the core textbook, one of the best-selling books at that time, was in the students' view encyclopedic in nature and uninteresting. Therefore, they frequently chose not to read it. The two readers, one with selections from primary sources featuring mostly qualitative research and the other with a large amount of statistical data in each chapter summarizing previous research on a topic, were viewed much more favorably by students and therefore were read more often. So another factor in choosing textbooks is whether or not we can persuade our students to read them. This may mean instructors will have to design "carrot or stick" assignments to motivate students to read if the textbooks themselves are not of sufficient interest to students to motivate reading.

Textbooks also vary significantly in the extent to which they integrate empirical research, both quantitative and qualitative, throughout the book. Some texts describe and cite empirical research findings in each chapter while others do so more sparingly. If a course goal is to provide opportunities for students to learn about or use sociological research methods, then texts that demonstrate these attributes of the discipline should aid student learning.

It would be a very useful tool for the instructor to have a comparative review essay of all the current introductory sociology textbooks available for introductory sociology including the big books, core books, and readers, as well. This would be a huge task for the reviewer to undertake, considering it would require content analysis of dozens of books, but it would provide a tremendous service to the instructor and to teaching and learning in general. No such publication exists to our knowledge. There are published comparative textbook reviews for specialty areas in sociology such as criminology, family, or education, but not for all aspects of introductory sociology texts, per se. Greenwood and Cassidy have published comparative review essays of introductory marriage and family textbooks (1986) and family sociology textbooks (1990). Both required an empirical content analysis of eight to thirteen textbooks for their respective courses as well as considerable time and effort. Tackling a review of introductory sociology texts and readers would be an even bigger, though vitally important, job. As the situation now stands, we are left searching for texts for our classes with what we can glean from our colleagues, published reviews of single textbooks, reviews that comparatively look at one or two concepts only, or what publishers' sales representatives tell us about their books. This is an area in the scholarship of teaching and learning that must be further developed, supported, and rewarded.

Resources for Finding Textbooks for Your Course

Time and time again, we find ourselves referring to that classic book, *Passing on Sociology: The Teaching of a Discipline*, which was written by Charles A. Goldsmid and Everett K. Wilson (1980) and is now over thirty years old. Many new resources for sociology teachers have become available since the publication of this book, including many articles in journals such as *Teaching Sociology*. There are also wonderful publications from the American Sociological Association's Teaching Resources and Innovations Library for Sociology (TRAILS), formerly called the ASA Teaching Research Center (http://www.asanet.org/teaching/resources/TRAILS.cfm). We know that, ideally, we should begin our search months in advance of the semester we will be teaching. To begin, Gold-smid and Wilson (1980) tell us that we should look to our colleagues, to students, to journal advertisements, and publisher's booths at sociology conventions as well as published reviews of textbooks in sociology journals. These are all good resources for finding lists of textbooks and information about each of those, but teachers today also have the Internet to help them with this task. That is a good place to start. Begin by looking at what books are for sale on Internet sites such as Amazon.com, Barnes and Noble.com, or other bookseller sites. Using a search engine such as google.com or yahoo.com is another place to begin. There are versions of "big books" and core books in online versions. Some of these are actually free to the user. While it is not our intent here to review specific books, we caution instructors to review carefully any book that they are considering using but especially online versions which may not have been peer-reviewed by credible sociologists who teach.

Textbook publishers have their own websites. You can find these easily by looking in any of a number of publications, but you can also do searches online for them as well. Once you have generated a list, contact your sales representative from each publisher and request examination copies. This can be done via phone, mail, website, or e-mail. Most publishers will send examination copies of books free, but realize that ultimately students pay the price for books instructors receive *gratis*. After the book has been chosen, it has also become a common practice among our colleagues to sell the "unchosen" examination copies to used-book vendors. This has a number of pros and cons. Instructors sell books to a used-book seller who in turn will sell the book to a vendor who, in turn, sells the book to students at a price reduced from the cost of a new book. Many argue that by selling these books to used-book buyers, they are making more readily available used, cheaper copies to students. Publishers, on the other hand, argue that this practice drives up the cost of textbooks not only because the publisher must recoup the cost of the *gratis* copy of the book, but also because they lose a potential sale to the student who purchases the copy from the used-book buyer. Ultimately, those students purchasing new copies directly from the publisher pay for the free copy that went from the instructor through a used-book buyer to a student. While this is a matter of personal judgment, it seems more appropriate to return these to the publisher and/or give them to students (if they are not instructor's versions) or libraries for supplementary reading. In our view, when requesting a book be sent to an instructor without charge for course adoption consideration (i.e., the instructor initiated the request) it seems unethical to profit from selling it to a vendor who competes with the publisher. This can only inflate the cost of textbooks for students in the long run. Moreover, if you are new to teaching this course, you may want to keep several of the books as resources for ideas for lecture, discussion, or class activities. Especially the ancillary materials (the instructor's manual and student study guide) can be helpful resources for you in course preparation.

What Do Textbooks Offer?

Goldsmid and Wilson (1980) tell us that course readings are important to teaching and learning in four different ways. First, the text tells students something about how the instructor has structured the course. Second, textbooks can be an important tool in changing teaching strategies and/or objectives in a course. Any veteran teacher can tell you that when a new book is used, it shakes up the old routines of teaching and makes you think about new ways of structuring learning opportunities for students. Third, reading assignments get at course integration in a way that lectures, discussions, or fragmented assignments might not. Students can almost always use help with this integrative process. Fourth and finally, students often read little more than what is assigned (if that much). Well-thought-out reading assignments can show students the utility of sociological material to their lives (Goldsmid and Wilson 1980). In spite of reasons for using readings to facilitate teaching and learning, some colleagues choose no reading or very little reading, or worse yet, make students purchase a book but do not reward students for reading or thinking about reading. Many of these instructors argue that textbooks have many problems. Let's examine the pros and cons of introductory textbooks today.

The Woes of Introductory Textbooks

An entire issue of *Teaching Sociology* (October 1988) was devoted to the shortcomings of sociology textbooks. Essays by publishers, editors, authors, and teachers alike were included in this issue examining the state of introductory sociology textbooks at that time. One publisher lamented (Graham 1988) that textbooks presented themselves as the "final word" on sociology and as such provided a formula for other textbooks to be written in the future. Graham describes introductory sociology textbooks as providing a chapter or two of reading per week, a reading level at about ninth or tenth grade, a supposition that the reader has no pertinent background for the course, a litany of vocabulary and definitions, and finally, a standard organization around such questions as, What is sociology? How do sociologists do science? How do sociologists study culture? What is socialization? What is social structure? What is inequality? What is inequality by class, by race or ethnicity, by sex or gender, by age? What are the major social institutions of society? (Graham 1988: 360). The pressures of competition in the marketplace work to homogenize introductory textbooks into a watered-down presentation of the discipline, its major concepts, methods, and theories.

Others have commented on these trends as well. Perrucci (1985) made many of the same observations earlier, but added that many books have serious errors of "omission and commission." These inaccuracies reflect poorly on research findings in sociology as well as the diversity of views and methods in sociology (Perrucci 1985: 203). Westhues (1991) tells us that textbooks are noxious and the objectivity in textbooks is a myth and that they depersonalize sociology and make it difficult to show students the applicability of our discipline to their lives. He advocates not using standard textbooks in introductory sociology (an option to which we return later). Friedman's (1991) analysis of introductory textbooks (from 1975 to 1989) concludes that they send students three messages. First, they convey that society is overly structured and impersonal. Secondly, they offer ideologically liberal overinterpretations of society. Finally, sociological knowledge is misrepresented as "the highest knowledge" about society. Westhues (1991) calls for a revision of textbooks with more balanced approaches to its presentation of society and sociology. While these criticisms are twenty years old, they are still strong criticisms of the textbooks that are used in introductory sociology today and have tremendous implications for our courses. The books we assign in our courses are important tools for achieving our learning goals as well as shaping students' initial views of our discipline.

Most of these critiques were written some time ago. As of late, there are fewer published criticisms of introductory textbooks. Does this mean that texts have improved in the last ten or fifteen years? One more recent review of introductory texts examined the glossaries used in them (Best and Schweingruber 2003). These authors' analysis suggests that current texts use and teach vocabulary not cited in what they consider to be the three primary journals in sociology (*American Sociological Review*, *American Journal of Sociology*, and *Social Forces*). Words like folkway, ageism, and even "achieved status" have appeared in these three journals fewer than six times in any period. They suggest that texts are teaching vocabulary not used by contemporary research sociologists (Best and Schweingruber 2003). Are our textbooks full of outdated terminology? Even a casual perusal of today's text offerings can demonstrate that the same formula drives the structure and organization that seems to pervade many of the textbooks offered by publishers and authors today as yesterday. In fact, many of the most successful books have been on the market for ten or twenty or more years (Schaefer 2010, Macionis 2010, Henslin 2008, etc.). Moreover, newer books to the market still seem to follow the herd in format and organization, as well as content. (See Ballantine and Roberts [2009] for an exception to this trend.) Others have suggested that in spite of this common structure, today's textbooks share only limited consensus about inclusion and definitions of concepts (Keith and Ender 2004b). Does this mean that textbooks have no place or merit in the introductory classroom? We should not be too quick to throw out the baby with the bathwater. Many sociologists disagree with these critiques. Let's examine the opinions of those who are more optimistic about today's books.

The Praises for Introductory Sociology Textbooks

Goldsmid and Wilson (1980) tell us that textbooks meet the goal of conveying information well, even if they have other problems. While Baker (1988) agrees that managed texts are problematic, he sees many works of excellence among textbooks, even if most are mediocre. He finds a long tradition of many books that provide high academic standards of learning for students. He further argues that sociology has always permitted rogue textbooks including those he calls expository (those with a particular thesis about society) and those he calls books promoting active learning (Baker 1988: 382). There have been fewer of the former and more of the latter in the last few years. Persell argues that textbooks can "show how critical thinking is conducted" (Persell 1988: 400). Both Persell (1988) and Kammeyer (1988) assert that textbooks are not clones when examined more closely. There are subtle differences in how theories are presented in textbooks, in their receptivity to changes in the discipline, and the extent to which the books convey the "core" of sociological content. Moreover, these can be important differences to the instructors and students who use them. The pictures and graphs that are often criticized as being excessive can help students learn by reinforcing a point (Persell 1988, Schaefer 1988). Texts that provide citations within the text show students where to find the original source. They convey the timeliness of sociological research and demonstrate the factual basis of the discipline (Hess 1988). Ballantine argues that introductory texts show students the "core" of sociological ideas and meet the needs of diverse student populations (Ballantine 1988). Many have suggested that the real problem is with the discipline's lack of consensus on what that "core" should be (Ballantine 1988, Baker 1988, Keith and Ender 2004b). Perhaps we are moving more in a consensual direction today as suggested by research presented in an earlier chapter. Most importantly the standard textbook provides students with an overview of the discipline. This "big picture" can be lost when courses use only selected readings or books that can be conceptually fragmented and not well integrated. Introductory students often need the benefit of this "big picture" in order to see, for example, how the components of society fit together, to see how theories and methods relate to each other, to see the cumulative basis of scientific scholarship in sociology, and to see how topics of inequality relate to various categories and groups of people. Regardless of what type of readings we select for a course, we must never lose sight of who our students are and what we want them to learn.

Criteria for Selecting the Best Text for Your Course

It should not be surprising at this point what is important to keep in mind when selecting textbooks for a course. Students and their attributes are, of course, very important. Institutional and course goals should be decided upon *a priori* and taken into account as well. The characteristics of a course such as the class size, the room, and the assignments given need to be known ahead of time. Factors that affect the teacher's workload such as teaching load, research responsibilities, committee assignments, and other service activities are invariably important in designing a course and selecting the text that will be used. Finally, an instructor needs to have knowledge of the cost and availability of textbooks that are being considered for a course (Goldsmid and Wilson 1980).

One other factor that needs to be considered is the readability of a text for your particular population of students. Most colleges and universities have records of student reading levels through standardized test scores and/or entrance exams. While this is valuable information, it is surprising that many instructors do not know the average reading-level ability of their students. If this information is available, it can become one more criterion to use to find the proper fit of book to students. While there are a number of more complicated techniques that can be used, there is one very simple one that is very helpful. Over thirty years ago, using Fry's Readability Scale (Fry 1968), Geertsen (1977) devised a relatively easy method of assessing the reading level of textbooks. This technique looks at the use of longer or shorter sentences as well as the size of words in a selected passage from texts under consideration. It shows how we can assess the readability of a textbook for our students using a "quick and easy" method. While this method has been around for several decades now, it is timeless and can help an instructor eliminate books that might otherwise be too easy or too difficult in readability.

Greenwood and Cassidy (1986, 1990) compiled a checklist for reviewing textbooks for marriage and family courses. This checklist can easily be adapted to an introductory sociology textbook. To this checklist we can add some questions pertinent to introductory sociology such as the following: What are the course goals of introductory sociology? What characteristics of students and their reading abilities

Textbox 4.1.   Criteria for Textbook Selection for Introductory Sociology

Theoretical Presentations
1. How are theories presented in the text?
2. Do theories receive treatment beyond the initial chapter?
3. Are female theorists represented adequately?
4. Are core sociological concepts covered well? For example:
   a. Social structure
   b. Socialization
   c. Social interaction
   d. Social inequality

Presentation of Research Methods
1. Does the book have a chapter on sociological research methods?
2. Are research methods discussed and well integrated throughout the text?
3. Does the book adequately treat the scientific method?
4. Are citations given for recent, up-to-date empirical research?
5. Does the book have a moralistic tone or evident political bias?
6. Does the book provide data or evidence to support controversial claims when made?
7. Does the book consistently discuss the limitations of particular research findings?

Scholarship
1. Does the book provide current, up-to-date citations of empirical and theoretical research?
2. Does the book accurately describe this research?
3. What kinds of sources are primarily cited?
   a. Primary sources? (Scholarly journals, research monographs)
   b. Secondary sources? (Encyclopedias, newspapers, magazines, undocumented web pages)
4. Are controversial topics described fully and fairly from all sides?
5. How well do authors integrate variations in behavior by race, ethnicity, religion, age, or gender?

(*continued*)

6. Does the book include discussions and examples of cross-cultural or global issues?
7. Does the book adequately discuss both rural and urban social issues?

Style and Format
1. Is the book readable for the students in the class?
2. Is the format well organized and useful for student learning?
3. What features, such as boxed inserts or glossaries, does the book provide?
4. Is a study guide for the text available from the publisher?
   a. Is the study guide written by the author(s) of the text?
   b. Is the study guide useful? Are the answer keys correct?
   c. Does the study guide contain questions that are also included in a test item bank that might be used in this course?
5. Will the book be ready and available for students by or before the first week of class?
6. What is the cost of book and study guide for students? Is it available as an e-book?

Pedagogical Considerations
1. Is the book consistent with your views of sociology as an instructor? Will you be comfortable teaching with this book?
2. Does the book's approach and style fit with the course goals and objectives?
3. Does the book fit with the program goals of the course?
4. Does the book promote critical thinking?
5. Does the book assist students' development of a sociological imagination?

(Adapted from Greenwood and Cassidy 1986; Greenwood and Cassidy 1990)

are important? In what kinds of activities will students participate? And how much detail would the instructor like the text to cover over selected topics? Please see textbox 4.1 for a complete list of criteria and questions. Adapt this list to your own context, students, and curricular issues.

In this chapter we have discussed the advantages and disadvantages of different aspects of using textbooks in our introductory sociology courses. The ultimate decision about which book to use, as we continue to argue, depends on the instructor's course goals, the goals of the instructor's institution and program, and what instructors want their students to learn. We also hope that this chapter has provided fodder for future discussions and publications about sociology textbooks and their effect on student learning. In the next chapter we outline the basic components of a complete syllabus and discuss its various functions for the introductory course.

CHAPTER FIVE

~

Tools of the Trade—
The Syllabus

Syllabi have become a required element of most courses in higher education. Most of us think about a syllabus as the outline of covered topics and the schedule by which the topics will be covered in a particular course. Today, especially in the United States, syllabi have come to include much more than this. Syllabi present students with useful descriptions of important course information. They can set the tone and invite students to learn or turn students off. Syllabi are increasingly becoming important tools for setting student expectations for learning and classroom behavior. Syllabi tell students how a course will be organized, how it will be divided into testing units, and what the dates for papers and exams will be. More and more, students look to the syllabus as a document which will orient them and set expectations for the course. Below we discuss the functions syllabi fulfill in today's classroom, the elements of good syllabi, and their uses for teaching and learning.

In her review of introductory sociology syllabi, Ballantine (1977) found that most syllabi included course information, instructor name and contact information, required readings and texts, and topics to be covered in the course. Even more than thirty years ago, when Ballantine conducted her content analysis, many syllabi included other information such as grading policies, attendance policies, or comments on academic dishonesty. Most of us would probably agree that there are certain key pieces of information that must be included in a syllabus, but that there is also much room for individual variation by an instructor. Of course, colleges, departments, or programs may also have policies about what an instructor should include in a syllabus, but nowhere does there seem to be a model for the "perfect" syllabus that we should all use. That is, perhaps, because "perfect" depends on many of the factors we have discussed in this book including one's students, one's goals, class size, and so forth. Syllabi need to be adapted to fit all of these relevant characteristics.

Goldsmid and Wilson (1980) remind us that keeping in mind the audience for which a syllabus is written is important. They suggest that we might find useful distinctions between a syllabus written for students enrolled in the course now and one written for those students who are considering taking a course. Each might emphasize different aspects of the course. This may be especially true today with the online course management systems that most use, such as Blackboard or Moodle. Many campuses are requiring or encouraging faculty to post syllabi well before the beginning of the term.

The syllabus is also written for the instructor. The syllabus is an organizational plan and record of what will be taught in the course. It should include goals, objectives, and a schedule of planned events. It also protects the instructor as a written statement of course policies (Goldsmid and Wilson 1980). Another important audience includes the instructor's colleagues. The syllabus is a document that provides colleagues important pedagogical information about a course which they might build upon in subsequent courses and/or which they might use to evaluate, in part, the pedagogy of the instructor for merit, promotion, and/or tenure (Goldsmid and Wilson 1980). Audiences for syllabi, then, can be varied. They include students, colleagues, and the instructor.

Functions of Syllabi

The syllabus in today's classroom takes many forms and has potentially a number of functions in teaching and learning. What we write in our syllabi reflects our knowledge and our expectations of our students, our course goals, and our strategies for teaching that course. In the literature on teaching and learning, we have found five major functions that are useful for thinking about what to include in a syllabus for introductory sociology. We know historically that the syllabus was seen as a *schedule* for the learner and tutor or teacher. This commits both to a timetable for reading, discussion, assignments, and examination. During syllabus construction, the instructor must grapple with the hard questions about coverage of material versus achieving learning goals. As noted in previous chapters, trying to pack everything into the course and the syllabus tends to produce surface learning. Paradoxically, *less* material often means *more* learning. Even when the instructor has opted for less coverage in favor of more learning, there remains the difficult decision about what to include and what to exclude. If we consider only the instructor's needs and the content of the course, we have left out the key component of learning—the students! The beauty of online course management systems is that syllabi are no longer delivered solely as a one-time piece of paper. It now is possible to update and/or modify the syllabi at any point in the course in collaboration with the students. They can, especially with regard to the course schedule, be adaptable and flexible documents.

To address the tension between coverage and learning, instructors should begin syllabus construction with the end in mind. As earlier chapters have indicated, we must consider who our students are and what our learning goals for the course are. What should students know or be able to do as a result of taking introductory sociology? Lang (2008: 2) suggests asking ourselves, When the students walk out of the final exam or hand in the final paper, in what ways should the course have changed them? Only when we have determined how our course should impact students, are we ready to address questions about coverage of material, order of topics, types of assessments, and reading assignments. Each of these should be determined with the goals of the course firmly in mind.

Parkes and Harris (2002) find three other roles that syllabi have in the college classroom today. They delineate the role of the syllabus as a *contract*, a *permanent record of learning*, and an *aid to student learning*. Finally the syllabus can also be seen as an *invitation* to the course and to learning sociology. What we say in our syllabi and ultimately what students attend to on a syllabus have an effect on their acceptance of an invitation to learn sociology. Let's look at each in turn.

The Syllabus as a Schedule

Most syllabi outline the topics and schedule of a course. It is important for all students, but especially first-year students, to have a schedule around which they can organize their reading and study time. Increasingly students today have part-time or full-time jobs and many have adult family responsibilities as well. Levine (1999: 45) notes that these additional responsibilities mean that for many students higher education is not as central to their lives as it often was for undergraduates in previous generations. Because of the "juggling act" of multiple and often competing responsibilities, surviving in college, let alone being successful, is highly contingent on organizational and time-management skills. In Light's (2001) study of Harvard undergraduates, he found that time-management skills were the factor most often reported by students in follow-up studies as important to their success. While this study was conducted at an elite, private college, the fact is that both residential and commuter students at other types of colleges and universities are just as busy and perhaps even more so.

A detailed schedule of reading, exams, and other assignments is a tremendous study aid for students in introductory sociology. Most teachers put a caveat in the syllabus somewhere that dates may change with advance notice from the instructor, which allows for flexibility and serendipity when needed. Moreover, it is only fair to students to have a general idea of how material for exams will be divided and organized and when they will be tested over it. It also can be useful to help students see the larger organizational picture of course themes. For example, in introductory sociology there is usually a unit on social inequality. If these reading assignments and class activities are grouped together for a three-week unit, then students might better see the organizational structure of the material (i.e., how one concept relates to another and how all the concepts relate to inequality) and therefore be better able to grasp the material. The syllabus in this way can be used as a cognitive map of learning expected in the course. It is often a good idea to organize each unit by simple questions that will direct our inquiry for that week or unit. This approach not only provides a roadmap for students to follow, but hopefully sparks their interest in the topic as well.

The Syllabus as a Contract

Goldsmid and Wilson (1980) discuss how syllabi have come to be seen as a legal contract between instructor and student. Syllabi are the documents where faculty lay out their expectations for student learning as well as other aspects of student behavior in the course. Lewis (1995) states that the syllabus codifies the course goals. Syllabi, especially in introductory courses, should be specific about grading, attendance, and make-up policies. Not only is there a large difference in expected student behaviors between the high school and college levels, but there is tremendous variation from college instructor to college instructor even within a single department or institution! To assume that students "know what is expected" without detailed instructions is just not practical. Nor would such an assumption stand up to campus grievance procedures. As such, the syllabus is a *legal document*. Administrators will often defer to an instructor's syllabus when problems between instructor and student arise, so it is important to include expectations for students in the document. Some instructors require students to sign and return a portion of the syllabus stating that they have read the document and will abide by its policies. Others will begin the semester with a brief, simple quiz over the syllabus to ensure that students have read and understand it.

It is also important, from a contract perspective, for the instructor to abide by the document. For example, if stated office hours are Monday and Wednesday from 1:00 to 3:00 p.m., then students should be able to expect that they will find the instructor holding office hours at those times. When situations arise such that this contract time cannot be met, it is advisable for the instructor to announce any changes in advance in class when possible and/or post these changes where students will find them (online, on their office door, etc.). As another example, if an instructor states in her syllabus that exams will be of a particular format (e.g., essays), students can plan their studying to maximize their performance on that kind of exam. If changes need to be made in these kinds of arrangements midterm, then it seems important to at least seek student input on the changes, and in some cases allow students to vote and make changes by majority decision when appropriate. The syllabus is a two-way contract that both instructors and students must honor. This is another great feature of course management systems that allow you to make changes to the schedule and notify students well in advance.

The Syllabus as a Permanent Record of Learning

Closely related to the idea of a syllabus being a legal document, a syllabus is also a record of what is proposed for the course and what should have been accomplished in that course. To students the syllabus is potentially an important record of their learning. In today's transient culture where many students transfer from one college or university to another before completing a degree, the syllabus is the written record they carry of the work they have completed. It will often be used by other institutions when students seek to receive transfer credit for courses. It is not likely that all students bother to keep their old syllabi once a class is completed. And it is not uncommon for the instructor's copy of this document to be requested by a student or someone from another university (such as for transfer credit or sharing with a colleague). It is important, therefore, to keep an electronic or paper copy of each semester's syllabi for such requests.

Syllabi, especially in courses such as introductory sociology, are important as key pieces of information for building cumulative curricular programs. The introductory sociology syllabus tells upper-level instructors much about what students have had opportunities to learn in their first encounter with sociology. Syllabi also become important elements in department and program portfolios when programs and universities are reviewed.

Syllabi as permanent records are essential elements in teacher portfolios (see, for example, Bain 2004: 166–69). One of many documents a teacher-scholar should include in this collection will be the syllabi from all the courses one has taught. Moreover, it is possible to demonstrate how new courses designed by the instructor are tied to earlier learning in introductory sociology through analysis of syllabi. Syllabi from a multiple-year period also demonstrate how an instructor has adapted the course in light of new developments in the field and in response to assessments of student achievement of learning goals.

They are necessarily one of the most important criteria that are used to evaluate effective teaching (second only to course/teacher evaluations). While syllabi do not tell the whole story here and should not be used as such, they do provide important pieces of information for evaluators. (See chapter 8 for a more thorough discussion of faculty development tools.)

The Syllabus as an Aid to Student Learning

Beaudry and Schaub remind us that the syllabus provides "a framework for faculty *to teach students how to learn the subject matter*, not just *teach the subject matter* (1998: 1). They argue that a learning-centered syllabus includes most of the same information as a traditional syllabus, but also includes information about instructional goals and student learning outcomes. A learning-centered syllabus is organized to help students learn material in ways we have already mentioned, such as by grouping material (what cognitive psychologists call "chunking") in ways to help students see organizational connections between theories and concepts chosen as goals for the course. It is important that time be organized to allow for activities that promote interactions between students, student groups, and the instructor so that students can get clarification, ask questions, summarize information, and apply concepts (Beaudry and Schaub 1998).

One of the most important elements mentioned by Beaudry and Schaub (1998) is the inclusion of *learning objectives* in the syllabus. Other research suggests students also appreciate this information in the syllabus. Students wanted a syllabus to have as much information as possible but mentioned learning objectives as one of the important elements (Bers, Davis, and Taylor 2000). Many instructors in the past have simply neglected to articulate learning objectives for their students and therefore they were not included in their syllabi. Given the learning paradigm, it seems imperative that we share *explicitly* with students what we expect they will learn in a course, organize the course around these objectives, and then assess student work by the learning of those objectives. Most books on college teaching in recent years have suggested that course learning objectives are a critical element of a good syllabus. (Some examples may be found in Nilson 2010; Lyons, McIntosh, and Kysilka 2003; Weimer 1993, 2002.)

The Syllabus as an Invitation

Another important but easily overlooked function of the syllabus is as a document that invites students to the course and motivates them to learn what the course has to offer. Unfortunately, it is easy for an instructor to fill up several syllabus pages with all the required elements such as contact information, policies, and so on (see the checklist below) to a point where the tone of the document becomes at best scolding and at worst uninviting to the course. This is what Weimer (1993) calls the "silent messages" in a syllabus. The tone of invitation becomes lost in the long lists of "dos" and "don'ts." The overuse of "don'ts" in a syllabus can inadvertently send a message that the instructor views students in a negative light—perhaps viewing them as children who are trying to see what they can "get away with." Therefore, the professor has created a long list of "don'ts" in anticipation of students' inevitable attempts to circumvent the "rules." Thus, an otherwise warm and inviting instructor comes across as offering a class that is punitively driven and uncomfortable for students. Rubin (1999) calls these folks the "scolders." Most instructors who do this likely do not intend for this to be the message. This issue sometimes requires the instructor to walk a careful line between trying to be inviting and have a positive tone, while at the same time making clear policies and guidelines as well as tips for success. This can be especially difficult with larger classes where, without structure, chaos can reign. But it is a problem when combining the syllabus with so much other information such that tone clearly becomes secondary to the other information imparted in the syllabus. Different instructors and teaching contexts may require variations in tone.

Ken Bain in his study of the "best" college teachers suggests that one best practice is to create a "promising syllabus" (2004: 74). Bain explains that in the promising syllabus, the instructor first presents the promises or opportunities that the course makes available to students. What are the big questions it will help students answer? What type of intellectual, physical, emotional, or social abilities can the student expect to develop as a result of participating in the course? This amounts to an invitation to an exciting adventure in learning which the student can choose to accept. Next the syllabus explains the activities students will be doing in order to achieve those promises. These are, in effect, the course requirements, but by avoiding the language of demands the syllabus fosters a sense of student control over their own education. Finally, the promising syllabus summarizes how the instructor and students would together understand the "nature and progress of learning" (2004: 75). Thus the syllabus, Bain contends, is more than a mere statement of grading policies but rather the beginning of a dialogue about how learning would be evaluated over the semester. It allows students a sense of participation in the setting of high standards while encouraging them to pursue them. This approach to the syllabus builds trust between students and instructor.

McDonnell Harris (1993) suggests that our syllabi should convey enthusiasm for the subject. It should personalize content and convey intellectual challenges. Moreover, it should convey respect of students and encourage the possibility of their success. Harris also adds that it is especially important that syllabi convey the instructor's willingness to help students individually. This approach emphasizes the instructor's commitment to the students and avoids the problem of creating a sense of opposition between students and the professor. These are all good suggestions that can be part of our consideration of the tone of our syllabi.

Even the order in which the contents are presented in the syllabus can impact the tone. We suggest placing the basic instructor contact information first or early in the syllabus as it conveys a willingness to be helpful to students. An inviting course description that includes the "promises" of what the course will deliver should also be toward the beginning of the syllabus. Saving the inevitable and necessary course and university policies toward the middle or the end of the syllabus, after the inviting tone has been established, is also a good idea. Such "rules" will seem more like "advice" from a friend along for the journey rather than "orders" from a boss after the friendly, inviting tone has been established. While the schedule of class sessions and the accompanying activities will likely come last, they are important for establishing clear expectations and allowing students the opportunity to organize their study time for this course and the others for which they are enrolled. Students do appreciate a well-organized course and a well-organized instructor!

Another good technique is to ask colleagues and/or students you trust to review the syllabus for tone and other silent messages. Does the document convey the invitation to the course you desire? We think this is particularly important in the first course in sociology or any discipline. We want to invite students to the world of sociological thinking and help them be prepared to succeed.

Key Elements in an Introductory Sociology Syllabus

Goldsmid and Wilson (1980), Wilson (1990), Royce (2002), Altman and Cashin (1992), Weimer (2002), Lyons, McIntosh, and Lysilka (2003), and Nilson (2010) provide detailed checklists of what should be included in syllabi. Any of these will provide a very good summary of what should be included in a syllabus, but to quote Erickson, "A good syllabus, in sum, is more than a list of topics to be covered and assignments to be completed. At its best, a syllabus introduces the subject matter, gives a rationale for learning what is to be taught, and motivates students to do their best work. It provides an organizational framework that indicates major topics, suggests the relationships among them, and previews the order in which they will be explored. It describes how class meetings will be conducted and what student progress will be measured, notes dates when work is due or tests are scheduled, and indicates how final grades will be assigned. And it does all this in a manner reflecting the instructor's teaching style" (Erickson 1991: 86). We have provided our own summary of the key elements of a syllabus in textbox 5.1.

Will They Read and Use the Syllabus?

Getting students to read, remember, and use a syllabus can be a task in and of itself. How many times during a semester will an instructor be required to repeat information from the first day that was printed in the syllabus? If you ask most instructors, they will say "too many times." Most students get four to six different syllabi during the first week of classes and many may not read them carefully or at all. Or they may lose them entirely. One task as an instructor is to figure out how to help students in your introductory sociology class learn that the syllabus is an important document that they need to read thoroughly and refer to throughout the semester.

Textbox 5.1.   Key Elements in a College Syllabus

1. Course Information: Course name, numbers, credit hours, time, and place
2. Instructor Information: Preferred title, name, office location, phone, e-mail, fax
3. Instructor Office Hours: Days, time, and place
4. Course Description: You may include the one from the catalogue and/or a more detailed one if appropriate. Include prerequisite courses/skills needed to take the course.
5. Information about what requirements the course satisfies in various programs
6. Information about how to access the course online, if appropriate
7. Course Materials/Textbooks: Full bibliographic citation for all reading materials including publication date, edition number, and ISBN. Include a list of any other materials needed such as poster boards, 3" x 5" note cards, etc.
8. Learning Objectives: State the course goals you will use to organize the course and their objectives. These can be general goals, but students will appreciate more detailed statements that include specific course objectives and some information about how they will be assessed.
9. Learning Activities: State the types of activities in which students will participate. Explain generally assignments and class activities as well as any outside activities that are required of students for the course and their approximate value toward the final grade.
10. Attendance and Tardiness Policies
11. Exams, Assignments, and Make-Up Policies
12. Grading Criteria and the Grading Scale for the Course
13. Methods (Tips) for Helping Students Succeed
14. Professional Standards and Expected Student Behaviors
15. Academic Dishonesty and Plagiarism Policies
16. Campus ADA or Students with Disabilities Statement
17. Tentative Course Schedule: Include a list of all assignments for each class session by day or date and topics and questions that will be discussed that day. Include tentative dates for all assignments and exams, especially the final exam as well as drop dates and holidays. Include also a disclaimer that allows you to change the dates in the schedule by advance notice in class, e-mail, or online.

While there is not much research from sociology on this topic, we can learn from our colleagues in psychology and other disciplines who have some interesting research findings about students' use of syllabi. Becker and Calhoon conducted research on psychology students at several universities and discovered that first-year students attend to different elements of the syllabus than do continuing students. Freshmen look at support services and prerequisites and attend less to information about types of exams and assignments. The authors suggested that this may be due to their lack of experience with the variety of exam formats and their subsequent study strategies (1999). We can take from this that we might aid students by helping them attend to these important items on the syllabus and also by providing handouts or supplementary materials about support services available on campus or materials about study skills and how to study for exams. These same authors also suggest that information on the first page is more student-accessible and therefore more often attended to. So if it is very important or high-priority information, put it on the first page. But you say, "It's all important!" So now what?

Several instructors have published ideas about how to help students attend to and remember important syllabus information. Smith (1993), another psychologist, tells us to staple the syllabus in the front cover of the textbook and ask students to do the same. His data suggest that this makes some mild improvement in prevention of lost syllabi.

Another way of avoiding the "lost syllabus" problem is to place the information contained in the syllabus in a course management system online. Such systems provide some security and can be used to limit access to the materials to students enrolled in the course. If the instructor possesses the technical skills, he or she can create a course website. In this manner the syllabus becomes more like a web page that includes course policies, goals, linked readings, additional resources for learning, and so on. This format allows for easy adjustments in the schedule without having to print and distribute new copies of the syllabus each time an adjustment is made. It also solves the problem of getting the information to students who are absent when the changes in schedule are announced.

Another example, mentioned earlier, is the contractual function of syllabi, which has the added effect of helping students attend to important material. If students have to sign a contract stating they have read and understood the syllabus and agree to abide by its policies, then be assured that, with a little prompting, students will be looking up their "rights" in the syllabus when needed. We have not seen any systematic, empirical data about this, but anecdotally we have seen examples where this seems to work. Raymark and Connor-Greene (2002) (yet other psychologists) gave a "syllabus quiz" to their classes during the first week and compared results of a second test later in the semester to a control group of students who did not take a test the first week. The difference between the two groups was statistically significant even though the size of the difference was small. The group that took the initial quiz scored better on the second test. The effects of testing a second time may be important to interpretation here, but nonetheless, it suggests that students might benefit if a quiz is given on the material. First it indicates to students that you value the information enough to test them on it. This makes it more likely that students will read the syllabus carefully and study it. It also reinforces the importance of this information when the quiz results are reviewed in class. This technique has a lot of potential. Both authors of this book have used these techniques successfully for a number of years and we recommend giving a syllabus quiz.

Weimer (2002: 84) takes the idea of a quiz over the syllabus a step further. She passes out her syllabus and gives students ten minutes to read and review it. After asking if there are any questions (there are almost never any), she gives students a ten-question true-false quiz on the syllabus. Once students have completed the quiz, she puts the questions on an overhead and asks the class to vote on the answers. For any that are close or wrong, she requires students to look at the syllabus again, outside of class, and begins the next class session by seeing if students have found the correct answer. Weimer argues this process accomplishes two things. First, it generates a good discussion about the class structure. Second, it forces students to review the syllabus for course-related information while getting the students out of the habit of expecting the instructor to "tell" them the correct answers.

There are a lot of great examples available of good introductory sociology syllabi, and instructors should feel free to borrow ideas from other professors (with proper citation, as syllabi are intellectual property). As mentioned earlier, the Teaching Resources and Innovations Library for Sociology (TRAILS), at the American Sociological Association, has published multiple editions of syllabi sets and course materials for the introductory sociology course. The sixth edition edited by Sikora and Mbugua (2004) is called *Introductory Sociology Resource Manual*. It is available in an e-book format that can be quickly and inexpensively downloaded. (See asanet.org.) Always assume that the syllabus is the most important document that you provide your students, and never hesitate to look for resources to make it better.

We have examined two central tools of the trade in chapters 4 and 5. In the next chapter we explore the lecture as another tool and discuss how better-designed lectures can help students learn.

CHAPTER SIX

~

Classroom Techniques— The Lecture

Today's classroom is filled with a diverse student body. The challenge of an effective instructor is to provide a multiplicity of experiences and present information in a variety of ways that will make it more likely that students will learn. In this chapter we will look at what the literature has to say about one of the historically most-often used standard pedagogical tools. This is the lecture.

Do Lectures Have a Bad Rap?

Lectures have been a primary delivery method in the college classroom for decades, even centuries. Bligh (2000) notes in his review of literature that there has been relatively little change in decades in the dominant use of lecturing in the college classroom in spite of many opportunities to use new technology or pedagogies. In another book, *Our Under-Achieving Colleges*, Derek Bok (2006) criticizes the arts and sciences for being slow to move away from styles of teaching such as lecturing, which allegedly creates passivity in students and does not facilitate desired learning such as critical thinking, application, and problem solving. Even though lecturing is still a mainstay of today's college class, especially the larger classes, the teacher who chooses to use lecture as the primary mode of teaching is often seen as using outdated or ineffective pedagogy. Burgan (2006) writes that this "viewpoint also relegates the ancient and honorable tradition of lecturing to an *Index of Forbidden Pedagogies*" (Burgan 2006: 31). The predominant view seems to be that there are other teaching techniques that provide more effective modes of learning and better promote active learning, including group work (e.g., collaborative learning), discussion, problem-based learning, case studies, and so forth. To discover if lectures should be relegated to the proverbial dustbin, we ask the following questions about lectures: Is it unfair to stigmatize lectures as an outmoded teaching technique? Are all lectures alike in their consequences for student learning? What are effective lectures? When are they most effective? What are the limitations of lectures? If we do use lectures, how can we prepare and deliver effective ones to our students?

What Does the Literature Argue about Lectures?

Medical educators McLaughin and Mandin identify a disease common in higher education that they call *lecturalgia*. They suggest that "painful lectures" (from the audience point of view) are usually the fault of the lecturer as a result of poor judgment, poor organization, and poor delivery (McLaughin and Mandin 2001).

Many teaching manuals devoted to helping instructors in higher education suggest that lectures are best suited for particular kinds of activities. Brown and Manogue (2001) argue that lectures are an efficient and economical means of presenting information. Many authors suggest that lectures are good for transmitting information to large numbers of people (Brown and Manogue 2001; Bligh 2000; and McKeachie 2002). Some suggest that lecturing is a very effective story-telling technique (Leamnson 1999). Lectures can also provide a structural overview of a topic or issue. McKeachie suggests that lectures can summarize material from a variety of sources (2002). McKeachie also argues that lectures can provide an opportunity to present up-to-date information that may not be in students' textbooks, they can give instructors the opportunity to adapt material to the needs of their own students, and they provide students with an overview of important concepts or ideas for a given unit or topic. Finally, a lecture can model an approach to ideas, a way of thinking about problems, and how a scholar in the field would address this issue (McKeachie 2002, Svinicki and McKeachie 2010 13th edition). Finally, Goldsmid and Wilson suggest that lectures can stimulate student interest (1980). However, these benefits that derive from lectures are not automatic.

Other authors caution the instructor about the limitations of lectures. Biggs, similar to Bok, argues that lectures sustain low student activity levels which are a problem for student learning (Biggs 1999). Common knowledge also suggests that lecturing for more than 15 to 20 minutes at a time is a surefire way to lose students' attention.

Perhaps one of the most commonly heard complaints about lectures is that lectures promote surface learning rather than deep learning. As a result, lectures are discouraged as being teacher-centered, ineffectual modes of instruction that inhibit more desirable forms of learning (Trigwell, Prosser, and Waterhouse 1997). Roberts (2001) argues that deep-structure learning requires role taking which lectures rarely provide students opportunities to do. He further argues that the transmission of knowledge should not be the sole or even central focus of the teaching enterprise. To do so may actually serve to stunt students' intellectual development (Roberts 2001: 136). Leamnson makes yet another closely related criticism. He argues that although lectures provide information, they are not effective at changing attitudes (Leamnson 1999). Other scholars argue that student-oriented approaches to learning require students to create their own conceptions of knowledge and/or require students to change their conceptions. Most often lectures do not effectively facilitate this process (Trigwell, Prosser, and Waterhouse 1997).

These critics notwithstanding, lectures are likely here to stay as a technique necessary in today's colleges and universities. As state support for higher education declines, many public universities will continue to offer large-enrollment sections of introductory courses in a wide range of disciplines including sociology. They are cost effective, if nothing else. In large-enrollment courses, it is much more challenging, though not impossible, to use active learning techniques and small group activities. With the popularity of new technologies for lectures (e.g., podcasts, smart boards, PowerPoint presentations, and electronic handouts), we are, perhaps, relying on lecture as a pedagogical tool even more than ever. Excluding lecture entirely from faculty members' pedagogical tool kits may not be a wise decision. In spite of these criticisms, many authors concur that lectures are *at least as effective as other techniques* for providing students with information and explanations (Biggs 1999, Bligh 2000, Brown and Manogue 2001). They have their place in the pedagogical tool kit. Yet it is true that all lectures are not equal. Some are better than others. Below we discuss some of the issues associated with creating *effective* lectures that facilitate learning.

Lectures, the same as courses, must have clearly defined goals, and those goals must be made explicit to students. If we are cognizant of the goals we wish to achieve with a lecture, then we will be better organized, and it is more likely that students will see this organization as well. Most of us have attended poorly organized talks or lectures in one venue or another. What they have in common is that they are more like a random walk through a forest than a well-planned trip to a predetermined destination. While McKeachie (2002) argues against using a "conclusion oriented format," this does not preclude being well-organized and making the organization overt and visible to students. Effective lectures can be organized around one or more questions that the lecturer plans to answer through the course of the presentation. In introductory sociology courses, lectures can be organized around one or more "big questions" for the day. (For example, "How do we learn to be human?") By beginning with a significant question, the instructor can capture students' interest from the beginning of class and help them see how all of the content relates back to the issue raised in the "big question." Brown and Manogue suggest that lectures can be organized around problems (e.g., "Why does inequality persist?"). They can be ordered sequentially or developmentally (e.g., "How do we learn the content of culture? What are the socialization processes used to learn? How does this learning shape our behavior patterns?"). Lectures can also be organized as presentations about comparative views on two theoretical perspectives, or they can be organized around a thesis or research question such as "Do women earn less than men in the United States today?" (Goldsmid and Wilson 1980, Brown and Manogue 2001, Bligh 2000).

Another issue in designing effective lectures requires becoming aware of students' note-taking skills. Some authors argue that students should be forced to take their own notes (Nilson 2010, Leamnson 1999). Others suggest that by using handouts with lectures, faculty will enhance student learning. But what kinds of handouts should an instructor provide his/her students? Some instructors argue that "full-text" notes of the lecture (such as copies of PowerPoint slides) are better for improving students' long-term memory of the material presented (Morgan, Lilley, and Boreham 1988). Indeed, on some campuses students appear to have come to expect these. Yet other research suggests that providing outlines of lectures with headings that include only main points may provide structure as well as activate existing knowledge structures (deWinstanley and Bjork 2002: 24). Hayes and Pugsley (2006) suggest that such use of handouts provides a framework for the lecture to be given. DiBattista's (2005) compromise solution is the "fill-in-the-blank" lecture outline. This approach is referred to as "guided notes" by Heward (2003). Heward argues that the use of guided notes assists students in creating complete and accurate lecture notes, increases students' active engagement with course content, helps students learn to identify key points in lectures, and ultimately helps students learn more effectively. We have both tried these techniques and, anecdotally, are convinced that students, especially first-year students, will learn more from a lecture if some kind of outline is used. We have also observed that sometimes giving full-text notes adds to student passivity in class and may completely stop any note taking. This is not desirable, if it means students are disengaged from learning in the classroom. It can be helpful, though, if instead of worrying about what to write down, students are focused on higher-order thinking skills such as applying the new information to a context or critiquing this new information using existing knowledge. Greenwood uses a hybrid type of outline which provides some information (lecture objectives, major points, and especially data when presented) but leaves plenty of "blank spots" for students to record additional information. Her experience suggests that the use of such notes increases average exam scores by about 5 percent. Howard (2005) has used guided notes in introductory sociology courses, which he has found improves students' note taking and keeps students attentive in class. In a seven-semester study of students in his introductory sociology course, 96 percent of students reported that they usually or always made use of the optional guided notes provided.

We cannot assume that our incoming freshman students in introductory sociology courses have already developed effective note-taking skills. In many educational institutions, instructors can promote greater learning by taking steps to guide students as they learn to more effectively take notes. It seems clear that, at a minimum, providing first-year students with an outline that includes lecture objectives and major headings for the presentation are essential components of effective lectures that facilitate learning.

Delivering Effective Lectures

We have already discussed how important it is in delivering effective lectures to have clear goals for your lecture, to be well organized, and to share these goals and organizational structure with your students. Lyons et al. (2003) recognize that lectures can be designed along a continuum as monologues or as highly interactive. All lectures are not alike.

Effective lectures have other qualities as well. Good lectures share with good speeches the techniques of good presentations. The best lecturers are good storytellers. They make their topic engaging in a way that captures students' interest. It is always a good idea to begin a lecture with an effective attention-getting device. Davis (2005) categorizes attention getters into those that stimulate physical traits (play music, show a sign with a large symbol); those that use novelty or incongruity (dressing in a costume); and those that play on emotionality (a story or joke). All of these can be effective ways to get students' attention. We are not suggesting that teaching is merely entertaining. But any good speaker must first capture and hold on to the audience's attention and then deliver the lecture in an engaging fashion.

One challenge in teaching introductory sociology, or virtually any survey-of-the-discipline course, is that topics can easily seem to be random and disconnected from each other in students' perceptions. An effective lecture connects new information with that of prior class sessions. Instructors can provide a brief review of what was covered in the previous class session and how that day's topic is related. Show students the transitional connections between topics. We shouldn't assume that all students are able to find these connections on their own.

Another important lecture strategy is to attempt to connect with students on an individual level as much as possible. Within the limits of the geography of one's classroom, attempt to make eye contact with all students. It is all too easy to focus on the students seated in a "T" (those students who sit in the front and in the center of the classroom). However, Biggs suggests that lecturers focus their attention on the "U" in the classroom (those students sitting on the sides and in the back of the usual classroom arrangement of rows, rather than the "T" where the better students often sit) (Biggs 1999).

Many authors advise us to do "change-ups," breaking up the lecture every 15 to 20 minutes with a different pedagogical approach to recapture students' attention and put them back into an active role (Nilson 2010, Biggs 1999, Leamnson 1999). Change-ups are activities that allow the students time to catch up and also provide them with opportunities to think about concepts and perhaps apply them. These include such activities as the two-minute paper, wherein students write reflectively on a topic in response to material presented in the lecture. There is the think-pair-share activity, where students write briefly in response to a topic or question, share responses with a classmate, and then report back to the class as a whole. An instructor could also interrupt the lecture with brief periods of discussion asking students to relate additional examples of new concepts as they are introduced or to offer insights from their own experiences in society that connect with the day's topic. These and other ideas to promote active learning can be found in *Sociology Through Active Learning* by McKinney and Heyl (2009) and *Classroom Assessment Techniques* (also called CATs) written by Angelo and Cross (1993).

Nilson suggests that students need time to catch up on note taking and listening and should be provided a minute or two periodically to do this. At the end of each lecture she allows students time to reflect, review notes, and ask questions (Nilson 2010). Instructors can also quiz students at the end of the lecture in an attempt to determine whether their lectures were effective in promoting learning. Another classroom assessment technique often used at the conclusion of lecture is the "muddiest point" (Angelo and Cross 1993). Students are asked to write on a note card the one thing from the day's class which they found the most confusing or most difficult to understand. The instructor then reviews the responses prior to the next class session and begins with a quick review of the most frequently cited topics identified by students. Regardless of the particular approach used to create a "change-up" in lectures, we need to heed Leamnson's advice that we provide students with opportunities "for reflexive thought about the content" (Leamnson 1999: 60).

As a result of the nature of graduate training and its focus on the details of research, introductory sociology instructors are sometimes tempted to be exhaustive in our coverage of topics and/or overly detailed in presenting examples. Harp and Maslich caution us about providing too many "seductive details" in our lectures. Seductive details are interesting details that are only tangentially related to our point. Their empirical study comparing classes where students were provided such details with those who were not found evidence that the latter could recall more main points of the lecture and could provide more problem-solving solutions than the students who heard such details (Harp and Maslich 2005). This evidence from psychology courses would suggest that in making our lectures interesting, we have to be careful not to provide too many "seductive details" which could obscure rather than clarify key points.

Other advice includes having well-prepared and thoughtful, relevant examples for concepts being introduced or explained. An easy technique for engaging students is to provide a single illustration of a concept being introduced and then ask students to provide additional illustrations based upon their experiences in society. This strategy moves students from the relatively passive act of listening, to actively applying new concepts and insights to analyze their experiences. For example, the instructor could illustrate the concept of "role conflict" by talking about how the professorial role (similar to many occupations) sometimes conflicts with personal roles such as that of parent, spouse, or friend. Then the class could be challenged to illustrate how and when students sometimes experience role conflict.

Another strategy for strengthening lectures is to use appropriate visual aids, especially for the details and visual components of your presentation. PowerPoint presentations are very popular in today's classroom and, as often is the case with newer technologies used in the classroom, there is a tendency to assume that if you use it, then it will improve learning. However, there is little empirical evidence that using newer technologies (e.g., PowerPoint presentations or document cameras) necessarily enhances student learning any more than using overhead projectors or chalkboards. Yet, because of all the bells and whistles such technology provides, we are tempted to assume that newer technologies will enhance our lectures and improve learning. Certainly the average college student is more attuned to such technology and for this reason alone it may be a valuable tool. However, PowerPoint presentations should be used thoughtfully and carefully to present information in a visual way that will complement the speaker and not detract from him or her. Teaching with pictures or images as illustrative devices can enhance student learning (Madison 2004). In teaching history courses Professor Madison uses photographs (some he has taken himself) to grab student attention and facilitate discussion, as well as to help students learn to observe rather than just look at an image.

Obtrusive sound effects and animations can easily detract from an effective lecture. The animation, rather than the point being discussed, can easily become the students' focus of attention. However, animating slides so that only one point at a time is revealed can be very helpful and keep students from busily copying the entire slide while you are talking about the first line on the slide.

Instructors should avoid putting too much information on any one slide. The typical advice is no more than six lines of text with six words per line. Always use font styles that are easily read in sufficiently large size to make them easily visible from the back of the classroom. Red, brown, yellow, or green text often is not easily visible in the back of larger classrooms. Font sizes smaller than 28 may not be readable for all students. It is a good idea to try out different styles, sizes, and colors of fonts on a few slides in the actual classrooms where you will be teaching before the first day of class so that you know what standards to use. This is especially important when teaching very large classes of students, and the optimum font style and size will vary from classroom to classroom depending on such characteristics as room size, lighting, or seating arrangement.

Finally, effective lectures should restate important points, summarize, and make conclusions clear. These rules are the same as those for giving any presentation. Research from the psychology of learning suggests that the "spacing effect" can be useful to helping students learn by repeating important ideas and concepts at multiple points in time within a single lecture and across multiple lectures. This, in combination with providing various examples from multiple contexts, enhances "encoding variability" and may improve long-term learning as well as understanding "of the broader relevance of the concepts" (deWinstanley and Bjork 2002: 24).

However, it is always a good idea to seek feedback from students. Having students write out their unanswered questions or the "muddiest point" (see this technique above) at the end of the lecture will provide very useful information to the teacher. This information then provides clear opportunities for discussion and review of important issues at the beginning of the next class session.

Thoughtful, well-organized lectures are an effective pedagogical tool for presenting information to students. Undoubtedly, many faculty members will continue to rely on this technique in the future at least in part in spite of other pedagogies and technologies. Burgan suggests that we use teaching techniques that fit our students' developmental stage, and moreover, that freshmen may not be developmentally ready for seminars, independent learning, and discussions (Burgan 2006). Lectures should be but one item in the teachers' tool kit. Good teachers need to have many tools to reach diverse student learners. Moreover, it is not useful to assume that first-year students are any more ready to learn from lecture than they are seminars and discussion-based modes of instruction. This is certainly a place where no one type fits all.

It is always important that students be provided with many opportunities to learn new information. This means if they read the text or assigned readings, hear a lecture in class, visualize the important points with slides, write down essential ideas in their lecture notes, and complete a workbook or assignment with the new material, they will have been provided a variety of opportunities to learn and review material. This will assist many different types of learners in acquiring new information and learning how to use it.

In this chapter we have discussed the pros and cons of lecturing and reviewed the research on the use of lectures in pedagogy and learning. Chapter 7 provides us the opportunity to look at another time-honored teaching technique—the discussion.

CHAPTER SEVEN

~

Getting Students to Talk—
Leading Better Discussions

You sense that the attention of the class is flagging. Students are slumping down into their seats. A few are attempting to send text messages covertly. A couple of students even have their heads down on their desk tops. You realize that you've been doing all the talking for an extended period and you're on the point of losing the class entirely. On the spur of the moment you decide it's time to switch gears in order to regain students' attention and re-energize the class session. So you ask what you think is a compelling and controversial question in order to engage students in a discussion of today's topic. Your efforts are met with blank stares. Students are now shifting uncomfortably in their seats, avoiding eye contact lest you call upon them. You repeat the question only to be met with what seems to be interminable silence. With a sigh of frustration, you set about responding to your own question with a few pauses interspersed in hopes that a student or two will chime in to share their own perspectives. Finally a couple of students do speak up, but you're disappointed with their superficial responses. You begin to wonder why you bother taking the risk of releasing control of the class session with these attempts at engaging students in discussion. In some ways, it's much easier just to remain in firm control by continuing with your lecture.

If you've taught for very long at all, you've probably found yourself in situations similar to this. You're excited and energized by the topic. So, why does it sometimes seem so hard to engage students in a discussion that is a productive learning experience? Why don't they seem to respond? How can an instructor increase the chances that students will be prepared for and participate in discussions? In this chapter we will seek to answer these questions and offer some research-driven advice that can make class discussion both productive and enjoyable for instructors and students alike.

Discussion as a pedagogical tool can be used in a large group format that includes all class members. Alternatively, the class can be divided into smaller groups for discussion which then report back to the larger group. Perhaps most often, discussion is used as a momentary break in the lecture or usual class format which re-engages students' attention by involving them through active learning techniques. What each of these approaches has in common is the attempt to engage students in a dialogue, sharing views, and participating in a critique of the various perspectives presented.

Just as a quality lecture takes careful preparation, a worthwhile class discussion also requires careful attention and planning. While exciting, spontaneous discussions sometimes surprise us in class, most often productive discussions are not impromptu eruptions. They are structured opportunities that allow students the opportunity to prepare ahead of time in order to effectively participate and maximize learning. Moreover, we should not assume that students know how to prepare for discussions. They may need help learning good discussion skills as well. If effective discussion requires so much effort, why should we bother with it?

Why Bother with Discussion?

There are a number of reasons to make the extra effort to use discussion and take the risk of releasing some control in the classroom. Students' active participation in the classroom has been linked with greater learning (see for example Astin 1985, Johnson et al. 1991, Kember and Gow 1994, McKeachie 1990), the development of critical thinking skills (Garside 1996, Smith 1977, Weast 1996), and even greater probability of degree completion (Tinto 1997). Of particular interest to introductory sociology instructors, Brookfield and Preskill (1999: 8) argue that discussion is a particularly useful tool for developing students' sociological imaginations. They suggest that discussion can serve four key purposes: (1) helping students develop a more critically informed understanding of the topic; (2) enhancing students' self-awareness and their ability to critique their own perspectives; (3) fostering an appreciation for a diversity of perspectives; and (4) serving as a catalyst for taking informed action in society (Brookfield and Preskill 1999: 3). Note that each of these four purposes of discussion may serve your goals and objectives for the introductory sociology course. By engaging students through discussion, they become co-creators with their instructor and classmates of sociological knowledge and understanding. Discussion makes students responsible, in part, for their own and each others' learning. In addition, a well conceived and executed discussion can make a class more interesting and enjoyable for participants as it builds a sense of a community of learners. Yet, despite the many benefits that arise from using discussion in the classroom, there are also significant challenges.

Challenges in Getting Students to Participate in Discussion

Karp and Yoels (1976) first identified several key norms relevant to classroom discussion. One of these is the norm of *civil attention*. Because most college and university instructors typically won't directly call on specific students unless the student indicates a willingness or desire to speak up, students do not have to fear being publically embarrassed as a result of being called upon when they are not paying attention. Thus they can get away with paying only civil attention; that is, rather than paying attention they merely create the appearance of paying attention. Students do this by making occasional, fleeting eye contact with the instructor (too much eye contact invites being called upon), nodding their head, writing occasional notes, laughing at the instructor's attempts to be humorous, and so on. Karp and Yoels suggest this often happens because students define the classroom as a passive environment rather than an active one. In this setting, they often make the assumption that it is the instructor's job to prepare for class and make certain things happen as they should. Students merely need to be present, observe the instructor, and passively absorb the information presented. Paying civil attention is one result of students' definition of the classroom as a passive environment.

Another norm which describes what frequently happens during class discussions is the *consolidation of responsibility*. Through their observational research Karp and Yoels (1976) discovered, and other research has confirmed (see for example Howard, Zoeller, and Pratt 2006; Howard 2002; Howard, James, and Taylor 2002; Howard and Baird 2000; Howard and Henney 1998; Howard, Short, and Clark 1996), that regardless of the number of students present in a class, a small number of students (three to seven) will do almost all of the talking. They referred to these students as "talkers." The remaining students become spectators to the discussion, contributing to the dialogue infrequently if at all. These students they labeled "non-talkers." Thus it is very easy for an instructor to come to the end of a class session believing a great discussion took place. But a closer examination reveals that the instructor and three to five students participated in a great discussion while the vast majority of the class merely observed the discussion. Howard and Baird (2000) found that one reason a majority of students take the more passive approach is a student-as-consumer mentality. When interviewed, several of the "non-talkers" justified their silence by suggesting they "purchased" both the right to be silent in class and the instructor's (not their classmates') expertise when they paid their tuition and fees. Unlike other class expectations such as studying and reading assignments, participation in class discussion was considered "optional" in the view of these students. In order to effectively facilitate a classwide discussion, instructors must challenge this normative assumption.

Effective classroom discussions require that instructors be aware of these classroom norms and take steps to redefine their classes to create new norms for instructor and student behavior. The first day of introductory sociology is very important for redefining classroom norms. If you spend the entire first class period doing all of the talking, reviewing the syllabus, explaining expectations, grading systems, etc., students will very quickly conclude that yours is a typical instructor-centered college course. Students will conclude that they are expected to be mostly passive participants in the course. Instead of spending that all-important first session reviewing the syllabus, an instructor could, for example, put students into groups to work on a brief quiz over the syllabus and the course policies contained therein. This process gets students talking to each other and establishes the norm that students must be active participants. Another strategy for setting alternative classroom norms is to have every student speak in the first class meeting—perhaps introducing themselves or a classmate (after providing them a few moments to get to know each other). This approach demonstrates to students that everyone will be expected to participate in class discussions, not merely the "talkers." In order to establish new norms for your course, it is important that you, as the instructor, don't do all the talking during the first meeting of the semester!

Who Participates in Discussion and Who Doesn't?

Research on student participation has identified a number of common patterns in college and university classroom discussion. The most often examined variable has been student gender. This line of research extends from Hall and Sandler's (1982) "chilly climate" thesis. Hall and Sandler postulated that patterns of interaction and behavior in college and university classrooms create a climate that is less hospitable to female students than male students. However, the extensive research into this question as it pertains to participation in classroom discussion has produced mixed results. Some studies have found that, indeed, male students participate more frequently than female students (Auster and MacRone 1994; Brooks 1982; Fassinger 1995; Karp and Yoels 1976; Statham, Richardson, and Cook 1991). A few studies have found that male students dominate discussion only in courses taught by male instructors (Pearson and West 1991, Sternglanz and Lyberger-Ficek 1977) but not in courses taught by female instructors. Brooks (1982) found the opposite pattern, with males participating more in female-taught courses. A couple of studies found that it was female students who participated most frequently in female-taught courses (Fassinger 1995, Karp and Yoels 1976). But the largest number of studies found no significant difference in participation based on student gender

(Boersma et al. 1981; Constantinople, Cornelius, and Gray 1988; Cornelius, Gray, and Constantinople 1990; Heller, Puff, and Mills 1985; Howard, Zoeller, and Pratt 2006; Howard, James, and Taylor 2002; Howard and Baird 2000; Howard and Henney 1998; Howard, Short, and Clark 1996; Jung, Moore, and Parker 1999). At best, we can only conclude that research on the impact of student gender on participation in discussion has been inconclusive.

On the other hand, student age has been consistently shown to impact student participation. When you face those long moments of silence as you attempt to start a discussion, it is most likely an older student who will come to your rescue by commenting. Research has demonstrated that nontraditional students, those age twenty-five or older, are significantly more likely to participate in discussion than traditional students, those less than twenty-five years of age (Fritschner 2000; Howard, Zoeller, and Pratt 2006; Howard, James, and Taylor 2002; Howard and Baird 2000; Howard and Henney 1998; Howard, Short, and Clark 1996; and Jung, Moore, and Parker 1999). The impact of student race on participation is a topic that has received relatively little investigation. In their study of introductory sociology courses at a large midwestern university and a smaller satellite campus, Howard, Zoeller, and Pratt (2006) found that student race did not have a statistically significant impact on participation in discussion. However, class observations revealed that when certain topics (e.g., racial profiling) were covered, non-white students became the dominant talkers because of their personal experiences relevant to the topic.

As one might expect, research has also shown that class size tends to have a significant impact on student participation in discussion. Multiple studies (Auster and MacRone 1994; Constantinople, Cornelius, and Gray 1988; Cornelius, Gray, and Constantinople 1990; Crawford and MacLeod 1990; Fassinger 1995; Howard, Short, and Clark 1996; Howard and Henney 1998; and Neer and Kircher 1989) have suggested that more interaction occurs in smaller classes than in larger ones. In a unique study, Fassinger (1995) concluded that student traits such as confidence, comprehension, interest, and preparation along with class traits such as emotional climate, interaction norms, and frequency of large group discussion were the greatest influences on student participation in discussion. Nunn (1996) argues that instructor teaching techniques (use of praise, posing questions, asking for elaboration, and using students' names) significantly improved the level of discussion.

What about the quality of students? Could we expect that our best students will also be the students who speak up in class? While better students frequently do speak up in class, it is dangerous to assume that non-talkers are poor students. Almost every instructor occasionally encounters the silent student who eventually earns the top grade in the course!

Why do some students choose not to participate in class discussion? Students give a number of reasons. Failure to perceive discussion as a student responsibility is a key factor. Howard and Baird (2000) found that students were virtually unanimous in agreeing that attending class, completing assignments, paying attention in class, learning material, and studying for exams and quizzes were all student responsibilities in college courses. However, non-talkers were much less likely than talkers to agree that participating in discussion is a student responsibility. Non-talkers define the classroom differently than do talkers and the typical instructor.

Other reasons frequently cited by students for their lack of participation in discussion include they have nothing to contribute, feeling as if they don't know enough about the subject matter, being unprepared for class, being afraid of appearing unintelligent to the instructor or classmates, shyness, class size, and feeling as if their ideas are not well enough formulated (Howard and Baird 2000). Intriguingly, in Howard and Baird's (2000) study a lack of interest in the course was much less frequently cited as a reason for a lack of participation in discussion. So students may be interested in our courses, but still not participating. Instructors need to develop strategies that can help students recognize that they have something to contribute, to help students prepare for class and thereby be ready to contribute, to create safe environments for shy students, to provide opportunities for students to formulate thoughts prior to sharing them with the class, and to make large classes feel smaller. We will suggest some effective strategies below.

So while we can expect that nontraditional students will speak up more often than traditional students and that there will be greater participation in smaller classes than larger ones, we are still faced with the consolidation of responsibility. Almost by definition, students who are more extroverted will speak up more frequently than introverted students. When an instructor asks a question or gives a prompt for discussion, extroverted students may figure out what they think as they are speaking aloud. In contrast, introverted students frequently need an opportunity to formulate their thoughts before they are comfortable speaking out in class.

There are numerous classroom assessment techniques that an instructor can utilize which allow introverted students the opportunity to gather their thoughts prior to speaking. Angelo and Cross's (1993) *Classroom Assessment Techniques* is perhaps the most extensive compilation of active learning strategies for the college classroom. One effective strategy is the one-minute paper. The instructor asks a question or proposes a topic and then gives students one minute to write a response. This gives all students, most importantly introverted students, the opportunity to collect their thoughts prior to being asked to speak in front of the class. It also reduces the chances that students who readily speak up will dominate the discussion to the exclusion of all others. This approach also tends to improve the quality of student comments.

Another popular classroom assessment technique is think-pair-share. Instructors offer students a question or topic and allow them one to two minutes to write reflectively about their thoughts or responses to the topic. Then students pair up and share their insights with each other. Finally, the instructor may then call upon selected pairs of students or seek volunteers to report back to the class as a whole. One good approach is to ask, "Whose partner had a particularly good insight?" This allows students to affirm each other before they are asked to report out to the class as a whole.

A third suggestion is to give students discussion questions ahead of time. This is particularly helpful when the discussion questions are tied to reading assignments. Discussion questions help students to identify key points in the reading and to begin to struggle with key questions and issues that must be addressed. By providing students discussion questions ahead of time, direct questioning (calling upon individual students) is less threatening. Knowing that they may be called upon also encourages students to read the assignments and be prepared to discuss them.

Just as there are effective ways to encourage non-talkers to become talkers, there are effective ways to restrain or control the participation of students who dominate discussion. A variety of very simple strategies can help in this situation. An instructor might say, "Let's hear from someone who hasn't spoken up yet." Or "I want someone in the back half of the room to give me a response." Or "I'd like to hear from a male (or a female, or someone who graduated from high school in the past two years)." These comments let the dominant talkers know, without embarrassment, that they need to allow classmates a chance to participate. In the rare instances when this approach does not work, a friendly conversation with the dominant talker or talkers after class can do the trick. Affirm the students for their enthusiastic participation, but point out the need for classmates to share the same learning experience that comes from participation. You might suggest, "I want you to count to ten whenever I ask a question. After ten seconds, you can chime in whether or not a classmate has spoken up." Typically, dominant talkers want to avoid alienating their classmates through excessive participation. By making yourself their ally, you can help them learn to judge when speaking out becomes problematic. Another strategy is to provide every student with two or three poker chips (or Post-it notes). When they speak up, they "pay" with the chip. Once they have spent all their chips, they are done speaking for the period and the rest of the class must assume responsibility for discussion. This approach also helps the non-talkers monitor their own level of participation.

Student preparation is vital for productive classroom discussions. What can an instructor do to encourage students' preparation? Providing discussion questions ahead of time as described above is one strategy. Another strategy is just-in-time teaching (Novak, Patterson, Gavrin, and Christian 1999, Howard 2004). Just-in-time teaching involves giving students an assignment, typically a short quiz or a problem to be solved, which must be completed shortly (say two hours) prior to the beginning of class. Most often these assignments are submitted electronically through a course website or course management system (e.g., Blackboard). The instructor then quickly grades the assignments, looking both for high-quality responses and common errors to use as examples during class. The high-quality responses allow the instructor to affirm the good work of selected students while offering a model and setting expectations for the rest of class. Likewise, examples of common errors (without attributing them to individual students) become a learning experience for the entire class and allow the instructor to correct misconceptions or simply clarify concepts, theories, or perspectives. A well-written just-in-time assignment can provide students with vital practice in developing and using critical thinking skills and their sociological imaginations. These low-stakes assignments provide the opportunity to develop skills which will later be required on high-stakes exams or papers.

Another commonly used strategy is reading response papers. Students are required to bring a short (paragraph- to page-length) written response to an assigned reading. These may be open-ended or be written in response to a particular question. Typically, it is a good idea to ask students to summarize the key point or points of the assignment and then to critically evaluate it. The reading response paper becomes a student's "ticket" to class and the discussion. It forces students to read the material and reflect upon it in preparation for discussion. Instructors collect the papers and quickly skim them, giving a few points or a simple "check" or "plus" grade. This approach reiterates students' responsibility for their own learning.

To Grade or Not to Grade?

Another way to motivate students to be well prepared for discussion is to grade them based upon their participation. If we accept the research and are convinced that participation in discussion facilitates learning and the development of critical thinking skills as well as the sociological imagination, then requiring participation is every bit as reasonable as requiring students to write papers, take exams, or make presentations. Yet instructors are frequently hesitant to do so.

One reason for this reluctance is the belief that we might be penalizing some students for being shy or introverted. However, using classroom assessment techniques such as think-pair-share, one-minute papers, and just-in-time teaching affords shy and introverted students the opportunity to collect their thoughts prior to being required to speak out. This creates a classroom environment which is much safer for introverted students.

Another reason instructors sometimes resist grading is simply the difficulty of making quantitative or qualitative judgments of students' participation. Keeping a roster in front of you and noting when each student speaks is one strategy. However, it is easy to forget to note contributions as you focus on what is being said, or, conversely, to fail to pay adequate attention to what is being said as you try to note which students have contributed to discussion. Additionally, there is the difficulty of trying to assess the quality of contributions, not merely the quantity. One could, of course, dispense with trying to track every student's comments and instead give more of an impressionistic assessment at the end of each class period or at a few points in the semester. The danger here is that such assessments are inevitably very subjective. If students perceive their participation quantitatively or qualitatively differently than you do, you can easily find yourself with a lot of disgruntled students on your hands bickering over the discussion grade or taking out their frustrations on course evaluations. Grading discussion is challenging.

One way to avoid many of these issues and still grade students' participation in discussion is to require students to grade themselves. A simple strategy for doing this is to provide students the opportunity to reflect upon their contributions to the day's discussion at the end of each class period and then assign themselves a grade according to an instructor-provided rubric. Here is a sample rubric for student self-assessment of participation.

1 = Present, but did not contribute to discussion.
2 = Made at least one contribution to discussion but did not read the assigned material prior to class.
3 = Made one contribution to discussion and read the assigned material prior to class.
4 = Made more than one contribution to the discussion and read the assigned material prior to class.

In the case of small group discussion, as opposed to whole class discussion, another point can be added to the rubric.

5 = Made more than one contribution to the discussion, read the assigned material prior to class, and made an effort to ensure that other group members participated in discussion.

This fifth point helps address the issue of talkers who dominate discussions by requiring them to pause and invite the non-talkers to join the conversation. It also provides an additional stimulus for introverted students to join in as their fellow group members directly invite their participation.

Rubrics similar to this one have a couple of advantages. First, it relieves the instructor of the responsibility of trying to keep track of every student's participation in the discussion and of making what are almost inevitably highly subjective judgments regarding the quality of students' participation, which can then be contested by students. Second, it serves as an indirect way of encouraging attendance in class. If students are not present, they cannot earn points for participation. Finally, at the end of each class meeting, this strategy forces students to stop and reflect upon their own contributions to participation and their own and their classmates' learning.

By grading discussion and making part of the grade dependent upon encouraging other students to participate, this approach effectively redefines student responsibility in the classroom and undermines the norms of civil attention and the consolidation of responsibility. Personal experience has shown that most students will assign themselves fours and fives for discussion. However, personal experience has also shown that those grades will be deserved. We do recommend when you choose to have students assign their own discussion grades that you rarely, if ever, override or veto those grades. On the occasion when students seem to be grading themselves more highly than deserved, the instructor can pull out the rubric and remind students how discussion grades are to be assigned. Grading discussion communicates to students that participation in discussion is a valuable part of the learning experience just as, for example, writing assignments are part of the learning experience.

Using Discussion in Large Classes

Even if we agree that it facilitates learning, critical thinking, and the development of the sociological imagination, we might fear that discussion and group activities cannot be done in large-enrollment introductory sociology classes. But there are strategies for engaging students in discussion in large-enrollment classes which have been shown to be effective (see for example Ballantine 2004). In any class regardless of size, discussion can take place in a whole class format, in small groups, or even in pairs. By incorporating at least occasional opportunities for discussion in large classes, instructors help overcome what can be an alienating, impersonal setting for students. Pausing in a lecture for moments of discussion also keeps students' interest and re-engages them in the learning process as it holds students accountable for investing themselves in learning.

Whole class discussion might be used as a way of responding to a brief video clip shown in class. It offers students the opportunity to relate the video to the topic being covered as they develop their sociological imaginations. Another strategy which provides an opportunity for development of higher-order thinking skills is asking students to provide illustrations or examples of concepts as they are introduced. This helps students see the relevance of sociology for making sense of their experience in society.

Small group discussion can also be used in large classes. Again, it helps make an impersonal setting more personal when students have a small number of classmates with whom they work on a regular basis. The think-pair-share and one-minute paper strategies described above also work well in large classes.

Maximizing Learning through Discussion

Sometimes students perceive discussion as a time to "tune out." Other students, rather than the instructor, are talking, so they falsely assume that nothing important is going on. Unfortunately, we inadvertently contribute to this perception. The lack of a clear structure in classroom discussion, as compared to lecture for example, can cause students to perceive that the conversation is merely meandering and therefore unimportant. Structuring the dialogue via discussion questions provided to students ahead of time can help overcome this perception. Instructors can affirm that these are important questions which will be addressed today and, perhaps, they will be emphasized on exams or in papers.

Students can follow along taking notes as each of the discussion questions is addressed in turn. Personal experience of both authors, however, reveals that students often have greater trouble taking notes based on a discussion than a lecture. One strategy to help students develop better note-taking skills is to use the board or a document camera. Whenever a student makes a key point or introduces an important concept, write it on the board or on a piece of paper projected with a document camera. Without a doubt you'll see students recording it in their notes! As the class progresses you may be able to develop an outline of the discussion or several topical headings with key points enumerated below.

Another good way to signal students when a significant point is being made is to overtly affirm the contribution. Doing this in an exaggerated fashion can make the point. "That's it! You've hit the nail on the head! Did everyone catch what Jessica just said? Jessica, please repeat your point. I want to be certain everyone gets it!" This approach serves several functions. First, it signals to students that something important is going on. It's time to pay close attention. Second, it can "wake up" and re-engage students who have merely been paying civil attention. Third, it affirms the student for her contribution while establishing a safe environment that encourages others to contribute as well! Finally, such affirmations reiterate that students learn from each other, not just from the instructor.

In order to help students learn to learn from discussion and identify when key points are being made, it is important to stop and summarize the discussion occasionally. If you are using prepared discussion questions, this can be done as you transition to the next question. "Okay, we covered question one. What did we say in response? I think we made three key points. First . . ." This approach allows students to review their own note-taking and gauge how well they have followed along. Do they have the same three points or did they miss one? Did they focus on the illustrations in their note-taking rather than on the general point being made? Summarizing reiterates key points, which helps students learn.

Conclusion

Classroom discussion is an important tool in the introductory sociology instructor's pedagogical tool kit. As with any pedagogical technique there are challenges to be overcome. Central to the success of class-room discussion is changing students' definitions of the college class-room. Instructors must demonstrate early on that this is a setting which requires students' active participation. The norms of civil attention and the consolidation of responsibility will not apply here. Instead, students are expected to come to class prepared, having reflected upon the as-signed material, and to be ready to contribute to their own and their classmates' learning. It is a challenge to redefine students' views of the college classroom when so many of their other courses stick with the traditional, passive definition. However, the rewards both in terms of student learning and instructor satisfaction are worth the effort.

Learning how to construct good syllabi, selecting the right textbooks and readings, designing and delivering effective lectures, and leading better discussions are some of the most crucial skills that a teacher must do well to maximize the opportunities for first contact with students in introductory sociology. In the next chapter we explore the challenges of day-to-day teaching and interaction with students.

CHAPTER EIGHT

~

Making Contact the
First Day and Every Day

For both the new and the experienced teacher, the first day of class can churn up the butterflies in one's stomach. Even the best, most experienced teachers often wishes they had just a bit more time to prepare for that first week of classes. Nonetheless, if your course has been well planned, you have an idea about who your students are and what you want them to get out of the class, your textbooks and readings are selected, and the syllabus has been written and is ready for posting or distribution, then you are probably ready to at least begin thinking about what you will try to accomplish on that first face-to-face meeting with students. In this chapter, we will discuss strategies for the first day of class, students' demeanor and our own attitudes toward students, faculty rights, how to respond when a class does not go well, and balancing our teaching with other responsibilities of the professorate.

Perhaps too often we spend the entire first class session talking about the syllabus, the textbooks, course policies, and so forth when we might do better to spend at least some of this initial period getting to know our students, finding out why they are there and what they would like to get out of the course. Anecdotally, some students have told us that they do not like the initial class activity which requires them to introduce themselves, and tell their major and something interesting about themselves. However, this approach may still be a good technique if you can get students talking with one another and learning about their classmates. It also provides you as the faculty member an opportunity to show interest in students "as people" rather than strictly in their student role. After each student introduces himself or herself ask him or her a follow-up question or make a comment that lets the student know you are focused on him or her. You might also use this opportunity to try to learn each student's name by repeating the names of all the previously introduced students after each introduction. The students enjoying finding out if the professor can learn everyone's name by the end of the class. It creates a fun atmosphere. Students occasionally have reported on course evaluations that this activity set the tone for the entire semester and that they appreciated the professor's effort to learn their names right away. Alternatively one could use a think-pair-share technique that asks students to pair off with someone they do not know, ask a few basic questions, and then report back to the class something interesting they learned about each other.

Being sociologists, many of us are inclined to collect data about our students. These authors are no exception. We usually distribute a short half-page questionnaire or 3" by 5" note card the first day where we ask students to voluntarily provide us with some information. Included in this can be demographic information pertinent to the course, background information about students' jobs or families, and whether they have had a sociology course in high school. It can also include open-ended questions that ask students to write down one or more questions that they have about sociology. In some cases, this can also provide a private way for students to share issues or concerns. This technique allows the instructor to get useful information (such as cell or work phone numbers that the registrar doesn't necessarily have) but it is also a quick way to get a short sample of students' writing. In addition, if students would like to provide this information, it can inform you of special needs that students have that may not be documented. Only the student can reveal such personal information to you. Other offices on campus may not, by law, share personal information such as special needs or medical conditions. Of course, if students provide you with this data, it must be handled with all the safeguards and confidentiality of survey data, but it also must be handled in compliance with federal laws protecting student privacy (e.g., FERPA). This means if you tell the students that this information is confidential, then it must be treated as such. To share it with others, even teaching assistants, without student permission could be problematic. The completed forms should be kept in a safe and secure place and destroyed after use. This data should not be used for any research purpose, unless you have students' permissions and authorization from your campus institutional review board. Violations of this could result in very serious consequences for both you and your campus. If you have any concerns about this, please do talk with administrators on your campus to ensure that you are in line with their policies and interpretations of student privacy laws. Better safe than sorry is the best advice here.

Demeanor and Attitude: Theirs

No doubt that student behaviors and attitudes are different today than in the past. Even if you are fresh out of graduate school, the students at your first job may be very different from those you encountered while a teaching assistant. At the other extreme, those of us who have been teaching for several decades may find students' lack of formality, casual attire, and lack of dress code remarkable and sometimes even startling. There is also a changing climate with regard to students' attitudes such that they expect to be treated as a "customer" of education. They may voice that they have paid for a product (such as a class or even a particular grade) and are entitled to consumer rights. It sometimes helps to point out to students that if they are "customers" in the classroom, then the faculty member is the academic equivalent of a "fitness trainer." The faculty member's job is to push students to become more academically and intellectually "fit" than they think they can be. If we are not challenging them to stretch themselves, develop their thinking skills, and foster their sociological imaginations, then we are not "giving them their money's worth" as faculty members! Reframing the "student as customer" analogy in this manner can often help students think about what they are getting out of their investment in college in a new light. But that the culture among students has changed there is no doubt. Given the costs of higher education today, it is not surprising that students often feel a sense of entitlement about their educational purchase.

It is not uncommon on many campuses for faculty members to work with students in a variety of contexts in and out of the classroom. Understanding what professionalism is and having clear limits about relationships with students is paramount to protect students and faculty alike. New levels of casualness among students today may mean that they sometimes engage in behaviors that we would never have considered when we were undergraduates—things such as wearing pajama pants to class; calling all instructors by their first names; calling you at home even in the wee hours of the morning; and "friending" you on Facebook. Managing one's relationships with students today can be a challenge for the college instructor. Moreover, there is much variation in the degree of personal informality desired or tolerated from campus to campus, but also from faculty member to faculty member. Most importantly, it is the faculty member's responsibility to set the boundaries for acceptable behavior both in and out of the classroom and their responsibility to ensure that relationships with students can be friendly, but professional. Take some time to discover your own values about this issue and decide (within professional limits) how casual or formal you want your relationships with students to be. This necessarily must fit within your campus culture, as well as with your goals as a facilitator of learning. Often, we have seen young instructors who rebel from the traditional degree of formality between students and faculty, and encourage students to call them by their first names, provide their cell phone and home phone numbers to students, and spend time with students in informal settings. While this is certainly acceptable within limits, it seems that the longer one teaches, the more likely one is to appreciate that there is a benefit to keeping a "friendly distance" from students whose work you must evaluate. Current research suggests that students benefit and are more likely to be academically successful, be retained in college, and graduate when they get to spend time with faculty outside of class (Kuh et al. 2006). Indeed, mentoring our students sometimes means that we spend time with them over coffee or lunch, travel with them to professional meetings, or even invite them to a family dinner, but providing students with open access to our lives is at best unwise, and potentially dangerous in today's litigious climate. Faculty should determine what the appropriate limits are for themselves within their institutional context and be as friendly as possible while sticking to them. Recently several of the students in a senior sociology seminar discovered that one of our authors had a Facebook page and asked if they could be a "friend" on Facebook. Not wanting to mix one's personal family life too closely with work, the one author (Greenwood) politely declined and suggested that she would be delighted if they would do so in a few months after they had graduated. Both students made such a request after their graduation. Now that they are no longer students, this professor is very comfortable with them having privy to her Facebook life. Both authors make it a practice not to "friend" current students on Facebook. However, this is only one approach. Some faculty members have attempted to adapt Facebook as an online course management platform, arguing that this is where most students spend a significant portion of their time (Young 2004)! Such an approach, of course, does raise concerns about security and confidentiality for course members, and you should be sure that this practice is consistent with your campus policies. Many campuses are now designing Facebook pages and encouraging students, staff, and faculty alike to join them. Young suggests setting up two Facebook accounts: one for your personal life and one for you and your students (Young 2010). Having a separate page (that does not include your personal friends, family, and off-the-cuff comments) may be the wisest approach here.

Attitude and Demeanor: Ours

In spite of differences we might have culturally from our students, it is important that we convey an atmosphere of respect and acceptance in our classrooms. Assuming that young people today do not have proper behavior, dress, or attitudes does not build a climate of openness that aids student learning. In the same way that we as sociologists would strive to approach a different society without ethnocentric bias, we should try to approach our students with a sense of cultural relativism. It may not be our world in which students live, but as teachers, we need to understand their world, respect it, and work within it with the goal of helping students learn.

We have been writing as if all college students today were between seventeen and twenty-two years old, when in fact many of us teach on regional campuses, evening colleges, commuter campuses, and/or community colleges where students can be any age and often are much older than the traditional twenty-something college student. Indeed, students may have family and work responsibilities that make their academic work very challenging. Being aware that students of all ages may have family and work obligations is crucial to facilitating their success. We must respect that they need sufficient lead time to complete assignments, that they may have legitimate reasons for missing class besides being ill, and that students' lives affect others' lives as well (such as spouses, family members, roommates, co-workers, etc.). The attitude we convey about our students' lives will inhibit or enhance the atmosphere we can create in the classroom and in our relationships with students. We should strive for a genuine appreciation of each student's cultural world and how it affects their learning. For example, we have both had many students who needed our understanding with regard to missing class or completing assignments on time due to circumstances that would not be acceptable in our upper-middle-class world. One student had to go to court (as the defendant in a criminal case). Another had to hide out from an abusive spouse. A third confessed that a judge had ordered her to spend the day in jail. We have had multiple students miss class (often final exams) because they were giving birth! Revelations about such crises often catch us by surprise and we cannot help but wonder if they are true, and usually they are true. These events do occur in the lives of our students and we can make their lives easier or more difficult by how we choose to respond to them. Our students' complicated lives also require that our courses are organized with assignments and deadlines clearly laid out in the syllabus at the beginning of the semester. Sometimes the best thing a faculty member can do for students is to be well organized! It is an instructor trait that we often take for granted, but it is very important for facilitating student success.

Professionalism also guides our behavior in other situations. For example, if one cannot make it to class or a meeting with students because of illness, a professional conference, or other conflicting commitment, it is important to give students as much advance notice as possible and/or make arrangements for a guest speaker, an outside assignment, or a relevant film to be shown. On any campus, but especially commuter campuses, students may drive for more than an hour to get to class. For them to arrive and have class cancelled without notice (in anything but an emergency) is disrespectful of their lives and schedules. When faculty members express the notion that their time is more valuable than students' time, it contributes to uncomfortable or even hostile relationships between students and faculty members. This can make it difficult to develop rapport with students and enjoy a relaxed atmosphere in the class that is conducive to a healthy learning environment.

When using a sociological perspective, we can't help but see the role of instructor in a different light. Our attitudes and behaviors toward students affect not only students, but other people who must work with them as well. Sometimes students will seek to enlist you as an ally against a colleague in your department or elsewhere. In such cases, it is very important not to criticize, openly in front of students, a colleague's work, class policies, teaching style, or other behaviors. Even if the behavior seems outlandish, to openly criticize a colleague in this way shows a lack of respect for this instructor and can easily lead to hostility between colleagues. If you have legitimate questions or concerns, they should be addressed privately with the individual first, if at all possible, or with an appropriate administrator. But be cautious about rushing to judgment. Very often students may be telling you only a part of the story—the part that puts the student in the best light and the faculty colleague in the worst light. The bottom line is that our individual professional decisions and behaviors have an effect on our colleagues, their teaching, and the climate of their classrooms as well as for staff and administration. We are all in this together.

Faculty Rights

In an increasingly bureaucratic college or university campus today, it may sometimes seem as if the power of the Ivory Tower faculty member of the past is no more. Faculty are no longer the ruling oligarchy that they might have once been. We are but one important piece of the system of education today. We may very well have less power with regard to administrative demands, and we certainly have less power with regard to bureaucratic decisions. Faculty still exert control, for the most part, in the intellectual realm over academic decisions, but only to the extent we are team members in the larger department, college, or university context. What rights *do* faculty members have today? These rights may vary somewhat from campus to campus, and these rights may be dwindling, but there are some still remaining. We have outlined a few below in an attempt to generate a discussion about them. Some of these may be considered controversial.

1. Faculty members have the right to teach their subjects however they deem appropriate for student learning. They may be held accountable for creating environments that nourish and encourage learning, but they can do this however they see fit within cultural standards of the discipline. But professors also need to recognize that the curriculum belongs to the department faculty as a whole, not merely to individual faculty members. Our colleagues collectively do have a right to know and even set expectations for topics and chapters to be covered in an introductory sociology course. Departments may even wish to require a common final or other common form of assessment of student learning. The faculty members teaching the course should have input into the creation of such assessment instruments. But such efforts, provided they are developed in a collaborative fashion, are not in conflict with the intellectual and academic freedom of individual faculty members. Intellectual freedom is one of the most important characteristics of a college or university. We must honor it. It is especially important in a country that values democracy and freedom of expression.

2. Faculty members have the right to have input on the selection of books and readings used for their courses. They may be bound by rental or long-term agreements, but full-time faculty should not be given a book to use by someone outside their discipline and be expected to use it. It may be that books are chosen by committee, but all full-time faculty members teaching that class should have been involved in the selection.

3. Faculty members have the right to be treated by both students and administrators with respect and dignity appropriate for the position we hold. We should always reciprocate this respect, but we should not be treated in any way less than courteously and respectfully.

4. Faculty members have the right to set high standards for students. We need to scaffold our courses and assignments to facilitate student efforts and learning as they seek to achieve these high standards, but challenging students is in their best interests.

5. Faculty members have the right to be human. They have the right to occasionally be ill, need medical treatment, or have family emergencies that necessarily take them away from class. We have already discussed the importance of giving as much advance notice for our absences as possible and having a backup plan in place for such occasions. It is not acceptable for faculty members to feel as if they can never miss a class, never be seriously ill, never have sick child who needs our attention, or never even take a needed mental health day. Know the number of sick days and personal days to which you are entitled given your contract. Use them wisely. You likely will not need them all, but guilt is unnecessary if you are truly ill or have another emergency. You will likely be a better teacher for staying home in such situations.

6. Faculty members have the right to ask students to speak with them in their office or after class especially in the case of behavioral problems of students in class. Students may feel threatened by this, but you can help to put them at ease by the way you ask them and by accommodating their schedules for the meeting. Not everything needs to be handled via e-mail or phone. We tend to forget this.

7. Faculty members have the right to have their view on student complaints or grievances be heard by the chair, dean, and/or other administrator *before* decisions are made with regard to outcome of the grievance. Ideally, the student should be required to talk with you first before going up the chain of command. Faculty should keep records of such occurrences in the rare event that these issues arise at another juncture. Many administrators are eager, understandably, to please students. Sometimes this right is overlooked in the name of expediency.

8. Faculty members have the right, and the obligation, to enforce the stated policies in their syllabus. If you have designed your course and syllabus carefully, faculty must follow through with stated policies. We all make occasional exceptions for unusual

situations, but overall, unless you are consistent in enforcing your policies, they will carry no weight and could become a cause for student complaints.

9. Instructors have the right to ask for help in improving student learning and their own pedagogy and teaching style. If it does not feel emotionally or professionally "safe" to ask one's colleagues in one's own department for help, faculty can look to the professionals at the campus center for teaching and learning, to professional organizations which often offer teaching-related workshops and conference sessions, mentors at other campuses and institutions, and the Peer Mentor program of the American Sociological Association's Department Review Group. The ASA can set you up with a mentor (at no charge) with whom you can talk to personally, by e-mail, by phone, or by video phone such as Skype. The Teaching Sociology discussion group is another source for finding assistance. While this is a public online forum, you can ask to e-mail individuals who post there directly for a more private conversation. We also suggest that you join the Section on Teaching and Learning in Sociology (STLS) of ASA where you will find many individuals who have dedicated themselves to enhancing teaching and learning in sociology. The STLS meets at the annual ASA meetings and they sponsor many teaching-related events. It is a great place to meet others who care about teaching and helping students learn as much as you do. You will find a similar group of colleagues and sessions at your regional sociology meetings as well.

What to Do the Day After

We have all had days when our class did not go well, when we could have handled a situation better, or when we made judgments too soon and acted on them before getting the whole story from students. We all have had bad days when our lecture or class activity could have been a bit better (or a lot better). It is hard in today's technological world to always live up to a "Disney" set of expectations to "dazzle" and entertain students in each and every class session.

After years of teaching experience, if you know you were in the wrong about something that happened in your class, we've learned that it is important to own up to it with students, apologize, find a suitable alternative, and then move on. Such honesty demonstrates to students your humanness and that you can learn from your mistakes, too. It also can show that you set high standards for your own behavior and that you are open to learning how to improve. Students may see this as being a good role model.

Likely the first few classes one teaches will not go perfectly. Often we want to make a lot of changes after we teach a new class. Some of the better teachers change something every time they teach. Adapting to new students, incorporating current events, or adjusting to programmatic changes at your college may mean that you have to change the learning objectives, content, or skills you want to teach in your classes as well. We believe that good teaching means accommodating such changes that facilitate student learning.

Balancing Excellence in Teaching with Other Responsibilities

Excellence in teaching necessarily takes time and energy. Most full-time faculty at four-year colleges and universities (and increasingly at two-year colleges) are expected to write research proposals, conduct research, publish regularly, attend professional conferences, serve on one or more committees, and do community and/or professional service. Teaching is just one of many jobs the professor must perform. How in the world is a professor supposed to manage his/her time well?

No doubt the reward structure in higher education favors research publications and grants acquisitions. And these are important functions of faculty positions, especially at research-intensive campuses. In *Scholarship Reconsidered: Priorities of the Professoriate*, Ernest Boyer (1990) suggested that this reward structure was too narrow and did not reward many of the other kinds of work that faculty members do. He even had the audacity to suggest that teaching was a kind of scholarship that should be recognized, public- and peer-reviewed. While his message was heard loud and clear in academe at the time, we really haven't progressed much in changing this reward structure, except maybe in one way. Now, especially in sociology, it is possible to publish research related to our teaching and our students' learning. This research contributes to a body of literature referred to as the Scholarship of Teaching and Learning (SoTL) in higher education. Over the past twenty years, many new journals and online sources have arisen which publish such empirical research. This body of literature has progressed beyond the days of "show-and-tell" where instructors talk about their experiences in the classroom reflexively. This area of research has grown to include quantitative and qualitative empirical research which has application to the teaching and learning. Within sociology, of course, we have *Teaching Sociology*, but there are other venues for publishing on teaching as well. These are listed in the appendix.

We suggest new teachers start out by keeping a personal journal about one's teaching. Regularly write down your thoughts about what went well and what did not. At the end of the term or year, look for patterns. What could you be doing differently? How are you measuring student learning and success in your class? You can review the existing literature on topics related to your own issues and go from there. It is possible to build a research project with publishable findings based on ideas you have from your own classroom. While not all SoTL research begins this way, such reflection will help you be a better teacher.

Whether you are interested in publishing or not, the best advice we can give new teachers is to take good notes about what you do in the classroom. Many instructors teach some courses only once a year or even every two or three years. You may think you will remember what you want to do next time, but a year or two later you won't have the detail of good notes that help you plan this course again and make the changes you desire.

In this chapter we have discussed some everyday issues of teaching which can loom huge in our vision if not handled well. We have discussed student demeanor and our own attitudes as they might affect the learning environment. We have suggested a few faculty rights to help guide your path. And we have discussed finding a mentor and publishing in SoTL. In chapter 9, we look at faculty development and how we can continue, day in and day out, becoming the best teachers we can be.

CHAPTER NINE

~

Faculty Development

Improving Teaching and Learning in Introductory Sociology

As an unabashed feminist who frequently spends time in class convincing students that they really are feminists but just don't know it, one of the authors was stunned when a student wrote on a course evaluation, "Dr. Howard thinks all women should be barefoot, pregnant, and in the kitchen." Even though Howard received that comment over a decade ago, it still rings in his head and stings. What could he have possibly said or done that led a student to draw this conclusion? What did the student hear or "mis-hear" that caused him or her to draw such a bizarre conclusion? We are certain that Howard was not the first, or the last, faculty member to ask such questions about students' comments in course evaluations.

For some, students' standardized evaluations of faculty and courses are a source of much dread and discouragement. We pour ourselves into our courses, giving our best efforts to students in the hope of facilitating learning; yet, in the context of an anonymous survey, students occasionally may be harsh, unforgiving, and even completely illogical. This sometimes causes faculty members to refuse to even look at their standardized evaluations or to have someone else screen them first, and remove the most hurtful comments prior to reading them. Yet, student course evaluations are intended to be a source of feedback that can help us improve as teachers. They are one of multiple ways of gathering feedback which can facilitate our professional development and greater student learning in introductory sociology. Standardized student ratings are just one way to measure teaching and learning. In this chapter we will discuss how to improve one's teaching and student learning through student evaluations (even when they are hurtful) and peer review of teaching. We will also discuss the use of classroom assessment techniques as a means of tracking student learning and improving our teaching.

Using Standardized Student Ratings of Instructors and Courses

Standardized student ratings of instructors and courses are commonplace in higher education. They are also one of the most often studied aspects of teaching (Cashin 1995). Yet, if you are like most faculty, you probably read them desiring positive ratings overall and hoping to avoid any of the "spirit-crushing" qualitative comments that we each receive at least occasionally. After a quick read, typically, we then set aside the evaluations and don't pay much attention to them until they are needed for a promotion and tenure dossier or teaching award nomination. Is that all student ratings have to offer us? How does one make the most of standardized student course/instructor evaluations?

Ironically, sociologists, like many other faculty members, who may be hardcore empiricists insisting on good data before drawing conclusions about topics in their specialty area, frequently cling to myths about student ratings of teaching despite significant research findings to the contrary. For example, some faculty members stubbornly insist that high course evaluation scores can be easily attained by being a "lenient" grader and watering down the level of rigor in a course despite research evidence to the contrary. Cashin's review of the literature on student ratings of teaching offers significant insight with regard to what lessons we can learn from the research. In sum, Cashin concludes that student ratings "tend to be statistically reliable, valid, and relatively free from bias or the need for control; probably more than any other data used for evaluation" (1995: 6). Likewise Green and Dorn (1999: 71) conclude that, based on their review of the literature:

Thousands of studies and several meta-analyses of those studies have
now been published, and the results are conclusive; carefully crafted
and administered instruments not only are highly reliable but also
validly measure the impact of teachers on student learning. (Green & Dorn
1999)

Yet, they are still only *one* source of data about teaching which
should be used in combination with other sources. In fairness, we should
also note that evaluations are vulnerable to misuse by poorly informed
faculty and administrators. Other sources of information include syllabi,
textbooks, assignments, exams, and peer reviews. Triangulation of measurement is always better than single sources of measurement. Ironically
student ratings are often used for summative evaluation (i.e., they are
used to evaluate your teaching for tenure, promotion, merit, or in annual reviews). They are most helpful, however, when used for formative
evaluation (to help you become a better teacher). Student ratings have
reasonable reliability or inter-rater agreement (.70) when there are at
least ten respondents (Cashin 1995). As the number of respondents increases, so does the consistency of inter-rater agreement. Likewise, there
is considerable stability between raters over time. That is, ratings of the
same instructor tend to be similar over time. Cashin (1995) further
notes that in studies which compare student ratings of teaching with
student scores on standardized end-of-semester exams, instructor ratings
were higher in courses where the students learned more as measured
by scores on the standardized exam. The reliability of student ratings
of teaching suggests that they are one reasonable measure of teaching
effectiveness.

Cashin's (1995) review of the literature also revealed that student
ratings correlate with instructor self-ratings, administrators' ratings,
colleagues' ratings, alumni ratings, and ratings of trained observers.
Likewise, student comments on open-ended questions tend to correlate
with quantitative scores on standardized ratings. Among the student
variables related to student ratings is student motivation. Instructors
tend to receive higher ratings in courses where the students had a
prior interest in the subject matter. This suggests that faculty teaching students who are majors have an advantage over faculty teaching courses primarily populated by non-majors. Expected grades also

impact ratings with students giving higher scores when they perceive they have learned more. On a related dimension, despite perceptions popular among faculty, students tend to give higher ratings in courses where they have to work hard (Cashin 1995)! Being an "easy" grader or awarding lots of "A" grades does not guarantee high evaluation scores unless students also perceive that they are learning.

More recent research has largely confirmed Cashin's (1995) summary of the literature on student evaluations of teaching. For example, Lo (2010) concluded student satisfaction was associated with higher rates of perceived learning. Agbetsiafa (2010) also found positive associations between student perception of teaching effectiveness and learning facilitation. Davidovitch and Soen (2009) concluded that the alleged correlation between students' grades and their evaluation of instructors was a "myth." Also consistent with previous research, Ragan and Walia (2010) found that faculty members who received the highest evaluation scores in principles (introductory) economics courses, also tended to receive the highest scores in non-principles courses.

Recently several studies have examined the relationship between faculty characteristics and student evaluation scores. In a study of faculty responses to evaluations, Kogan, Schoenfeld-Tacher, and Hellyer (2010) concluded that the feelings of female faculty members are more negatively impacted by student evaluations than those of male faculty. A study of faculty in a College of Education at a research-intensive university in the southern United States found that White faculty and faculty designated as "other" received significantly higher scores than Black faculty (Smith 2007). Yet another intriguing study compared the student evaluation scores of lesbian, gay, bisexual, and transgender university faculty who had disclosed their LGBT identity with their students with evaluation scores of LGBT faculty who had not self-disclosed. The results indicated that instructors' self-disclosure had no detrimental effect upon students' evaluations of instructors' teaching effectiveness (Jennings 2010). In sum, more recent research regarding student evaluations of teaching have largely remained consistent with Cashin's (1995) review of the literature.

If we accept that student ratings are, generally speaking, reliable and valid, what can we learn from our students' evaluations of our teaching? One thing that the quantitative ratings scores can do is help us identify patterns of strengths and weaknesses as teachers. Take a look at your student rating results, not just from a single course but from multiple courses over multiple semesters. On which item[s] do you consistently score most highly? On which item[s] do you receive the lowest ratings from students? Do students give you high marks for rapport in the classroom, but poor marks for organization of the course? Do students give you high scores on stimulating critical thinking, but lower marks for enthusiasm? Identify what it is that students think you do well and where you can focus your efforts for improvement.

We suggest that you create a spreadsheet tracking student ratings by item across multiple courses and semesters. Once you have organized the data, you can also begin to examine whether your scores provide evidence of meeting course objectives. For example, if helping students learn to think critically is a course objective in each of your classes, take a close look at the item[s] related to critical thinking. Is it one of your more highly ranked items over time? If comparative data are available, are your scores consistently above the department, university, or national mean for this item[s]? We all should be concerned with student learning. What do the items related to student learning reveal? Do students indicate they perceive they are learning a lot in our course relative to department, university, or national means? Is student learning one of the items with consistently high scores?

Another strategy is to look for change over time. As you have begun to think seriously about teaching and learning, have the scores on the items related to critical thinking and learning, for example, risen over time? Have the items on which you received lower scores risen over time? Have you maintained consistently high scores on items related to your goals for your courses? While the quantitative scores may not offer you specific direction for how to improve your teaching and students' learning, they can provide some rough idea of what you are doing well and what might benefit from some more attention. For example, if the item related to organization of the course is consistently one of your lowest rated items, you probably need to consider how to make the course more organized and make that organization more obvious to students.

Oftentimes, students' qualitative comments provide more specific advice. Of course, as noted above, qualitative comments can also be the most hurtful. Only recently have researchers begun to investigate student cruelty in evaluations (Lindahl and Unger 2010). Sometimes qualitative comments can be totally irrelevant (e.g., commenting on your sense of fashion or your weight). Despite the occasionally hurtful and irrelevant input, qualitative comments can be a source of tremendous insight for your development as a teacher. We recommend ignoring the outlier comments, both those that are harshly critical and those that are effusive in their praise. (Although it may help to dwell a bit on the strongly positive comments to balance our sense of hurt from the negative comments.) Again, it helps to consider multiple courses over multiple semesters. For what aspects of your teaching do students consistently offer praise? Do they report that your lectures are stimulating and engaging? Do they report that your organization of the course facilitates their learning? For what aspects of your teaching do students consistently offer criticism? Do they find some aspect of your approach to grading to be unfair or unclear? Do they ask for greater variety in your methods of assessing learning? Do they want more frequent opportunities to interact with peers during class? Do they express a need for greater organization or structure in the course? Do students comment that they learned a lot in your class?

If your college or university's student rating form does not ask questions which provide useful feedback, consider creating your own evaluation form. Create the opportunity to ask about specific aspects of the course. In designing the form, remember that there are some things which students are simply not qualified to judge. For example, students have no basis for determining whether or not the course or the textbook presents "an up-to-date synthesis of the field." However, for introductory sociology courses, students could be asked to comment on the development of their sociological imaginations or their understanding of the sociological perspective as a result of participating in the course. Students could also comment on the number and variety of learning assessments (e.g., exams, quizzes, papers, etc.). Students could comment on their perceptions of the effectiveness of small group or active learning exercises in the course. This type of faculty-created feedback could also be used near the midpoint of the semester to gauge how the course is progressing to date. The clear advantage of this strategy is that the instructor receives feedback while there is still an opportunity to make changes in the course. One caution though: If you ask students for input on the course midstream, you must be willing to take their input seriously and make changes. Students may become resentful if you request their input and then do not act upon it. Greenwood gave students a short questionnaire midway through the semester and simply asked students what they liked best and what they liked least in the course. Based on the aggregate results she made changes accordingly. Course evaluations can be used at any point in the course, not just at the end.

This feedback, tailored specifically to your course, could prove more valuable for course improvement than the institutionally mandated student ratings. For example, Howard (2005) used an end-of-semester survey of students in his introductory sociology course to measure students' perceptions of and effort in the course. He found after just a few semesters that only 40 percent of students reported that they "usually" or "always" read the assigned chapters in the survey textbook. Therefore, he switched from an introductory sociology survey textbook to two readers, one with an emphasis on statistical evidence and the second with a qualitative orientation. In subsequent semesters, he found that 75 percent of students reported that they "usually" or "always" read the assigned chapters. He was also able to use the data collected over nine semesters to determine that the best predictors of success in his introductory sociology course were class attendance and reading the assignments. He now regularly shares this information with students on the first day of class in an effort to motivate them to attend class and read assignments. In sum, systematically collecting data through institutionally mandated student ratings of instruction or through individually designed evaluation instruments can facilitate our development as teachers. While student ratings of teachers are one source of information and data, they are only a single source. Multiple sources of data always give us a better picture of reality than just one source.

Peer Review of Teaching

Peer review of one's teaching can also be very helpful for one's professional development as a teacher. Chism and Chism define peer review of teaching as "informed colleague judgment about faculty teaching for either fostering improvement or making personnel decisions" (2007:

3). For our purposes, we will focus primarily on the goal of fostering improvement, but the two purposes easily become intertwined. As Chism and Chism note, "informed judgment" implies that peer review needs to be a systematic act that utilizes appropriate evidence and investigation. "Colleague" implies that the review is conducted by someone who has appropriate expertise to provide feedback on one's pedagogy, disciplinary content, or both. In short, peer reviewers should be trained in how to conduct an effective review that will assist another teacher. One of the main advantages of peer review of teaching is that, when conducted appropriately, it can facilitate a dialogue about effective teaching between the reviewer and those being reviewed. As faculty members who often conduct peer reviews of teaching, we find that we learn as much or more about how to improve our teaching from the faculty member being reviewed than he or she learns from us.

The most helpful peer reviews involve a class session observation, ideally more than one—but practically speaking most peer reviews consist of an observation of a single class session, by the reviewer. Even if less than ideal, a single class observation can be very beneficial if done appropriately. Before the visit, the reviewer and the teacher may want to sit down and discuss the course goals, the syllabus, and other pertinent information about the course and the session which will be reviewed. Ideally, the reviewer has been trained as a peer reviewer, but at the very least she or he uses a guide or checklist to rate and comment on various aspects of teaching pedagogy and, in some cases, course content. Chism and Chism (2007) offer a variety of models which can be easily utilized. The guide forces the reviewer to consider particular aspects of pedagogy. For example, was the instructor well organized? Were goals or objectives for the class session explained? Were the goals appropriate for the course and the particular class session? Did the instructor demonstrate rapport with students? Did the instructor periodically summarize and review key points? Did the instructor seek to facilitate interaction with and among students? By giving the reviewer a list of criteria to consider, peer review of teaching becomes more beneficial. Ideally, the form provides for quantitative ratings on a variety of dimensions (e.g., 1 to 5), and also provides an opportunity to comment on precisely why a given numerical rating was assigned. The reviewer and instructor then discuss the completed written review in a private context where the instructor has the opportunity to respond to or address any concerns. The instructor is typically provided with a written version of the review for his or her records.

Peer review of teaching can and should include a review of course materials such as syllabi, exams, handouts, PowerPoint presentations, and major assignments in addition to the classroom observation. Reviewers can help the faculty member consider whether the course materials facilitate achievement of the course objectives. For example, if an introductory sociology teacher wants to develop students' sociological imaginations, do the materials serve that goal by providing opportunities and structure for students to develop it? Or do the presentations and handouts merely present students with the "right" answers instead of challenging them to process questions and issues sociologically?

We have found the best peer reviews are those that both help the instructor identify his or her strengths and identify areas for improvement. Often faculty members are so invested in their teaching that they have difficulty identifying what they do particularly well. A colleague's peer review can often help them recognize their strengths. For example, during a class observation of a colleague teaching introductory sociology, Howard noted that the instructor repeatedly introduced studies or quasi-experiments related to the day's topic that had counterintuitive results. But rather than merely telling students how the researchers explained the findings, the instructor challenged his class to offer hypotheses that would account for the counterintuitive results. In so doing, he gave students repeated opportunities to develop both critical thinking skills and their sociological imaginations. In the post-observation discussion, Howard pointed this out to the reviewed faculty member who was not aware of this pattern in his teaching. The review process affirmed him for an aspect of his teaching which he merely took for granted.

Sometimes criticisms in a peer review can also be very helpful. Used in combination with subsequent peer reviews, they can be used to demonstrate improvement in teaching effectiveness. In Howard's first professional peer review, a respected senior colleague known for her teaching excellence noted that the questions on an exam returned on the day of the observation were not written to facilitate critical thinking and assessment of evidence. This was the case despite a statement in the syllabus identifying development of critical thinking skills as a major goal of the course. She was correct, of course, to point out the inconsistency. That comment, in the written peer review and in the post-observation debriefing, caused Howard to take very seriously the goal of developing students' critical thinking skills in his courses and using exams and other assignments as a way of assessing students' progress toward that goal. In subsequent peer reviews conducted by different colleagues, facilitating critical thinking was highlighted as a strength of Howard's teaching pedagogy. Later when nominated for a teaching award, Howard was able to refer to the shortcoming noted in the first peer review to which he responded with changes in his teaching and the subsequent colleagues who found that what was once a weakness was now a strength. Thus peer reviews of teaching can be very helpful in both assisting us with identifying our strengths and focusing our attention on areas for improvement.

Classroom Assessment Techniques

In chapter 7, we touched upon some frequently used classroom assessment techniques (CATs) as a means of sparking student participation in discussion. However, CATs can be used for a wide variety of purposes in the pursuit of increased student learning. In their book *Classroom Assessment Techniques*, which has become the "Bible" of classroom assessment, Angelo and Cross argue that through close observation of students, the collection of frequent feedback, and modest classroom "experiments," faculty members can learn much about students' learning and how they respond to particular pedagogical strategies (1993: 3). The key here is to collect frequent, useful feedback about how students respond to particular teaching and learning strategies. The information collected can then be used to refocus our teaching with the goal of producing greater learning.

CATs are helpful, not only to the teacher, but also to students. They provide students with low-stakes assignments (e.g., brief written responses for few points) that require them to practice skills or demonstrate understanding which will be required in future high-stakes assignments (e.g., exams and research papers that weigh heavily in the semester grade).

Angelo and Cross offer fifty different CATs in their volume. Some are very commonly used in higher education, such as "One Minute Papers" and the "Muddiest Point." The "One Minute Paper" technique involves stopping the class and asking students to write briefly in response to the questions "What was the most important thing you learned in this class?" and/or "What important question remains unanswered?" (1993: 148). This technique allows an instructor to gauge students' understanding and comprehension of a topic. The instructor reviews the feedback before the following class session and then may respond to students' input. For example, did students grasp the main point of the day's topic or were they focused on a tangential matter? Did students misunderstand some key aspect of the topic? Do students still have questions about a topic the instructor may have thought was already thoroughly explored in class? One Minute Papers are a great way for an instructor to get quick feedback regarding students' learning without having to wait for an exam, paper, or other major assignment.

The Muddiest Point is similar to the second question asked in a One Minute Paper. (1993: 154). This technique is often used as a wrap-up to a class session. Students are asked to write brief responses to the question, "What was the muddiest point in today's lecture (discussion, group activity, active learning technique, film, etc.)?" The instructor can then review the feedback and begin the following class session with a quick recap of the previous session clarifying common points of misunderstanding or confusion. This strategy also serves a bridge from one session to the next and helps students get focused and ready for additional learning.

Angelo and Cross also offer numerous other CATs which are less well-known, but no less effective. "Empty Outlines," for example, is a technique that is particularly valuable when an instructor finds that students are having difficulty taking appropriate notes during a lecture or discussion (1993: 138). The instructor provides students with an empty or partially completed outline of the lecture (or homework assignment, etc.). Students must "fill in the gaps" in the outline. Knowing that they need to complete the outline, students stay focused longer and, hopefully, follow the logic of a lecture or an argument more closely, thereby increasing learning. This technique also results in better class notes from which students can prepare for exams and other high-stakes learning assessments. This is the underlying premise upon which Greenwood uses the guided notes in her introductory course which were discussed in an earlier chapter.

Classroom assessment techniques serve both students and faculty. For students, they can present low-stakes opportunities to practice skills and demonstrate understanding prior to high-stakes assessments. They also allow students the opportunity to provide feedback to faculty members regarding their learning. This information, in turn, allows faculty members to adapt their pedagogical strategies and their focus to better facilitate that learning. Over time, such valuable feedback will make one a more reflective and more effective instructor.

Assessing Student Learning

The ultimate goal of any college course is to assist students in the learning process. It is difficult to observe and measure teaching, but even more so to assess what students have actually learned. Many faculty members assume that course grades are an assessment of student learning. While this is true to an extent, grades reflect the assessment of a culmination of the students' work and are based on many factors including attendance, participation, turning in assignments on time, writing well on an exam, reading comprehension skills, and other skills not necessarily addressed in the sociology class. So while students' course grades are correlated with student learning, they reflect many other facets of the students' experiences in the class as well. Nonetheless we cannot rely upon assessments of learning in student ratings alone. Increasingly, accreditation organizations and other governing bodies are requiring colleges and universities to document the ways in which students learn (and/or benefit from taking a particular class or all the courses in a sequence). Therefore, sometimes as faculty we are asked to assess students' work in ways that seem redundant with grading. Yet assessment does not equal grading. Sometimes it may be important and informative to measure what students know at the beginning of class or in an assignment, provide an activity for learning, and then assess learning a second time. Using a rubric for learning both before and after the learning activity is essential for comparative pre/post data. Such data about even the smallest of activities in your class can provide a wealth of information about the usefulness of a particular teaching technique or activity. The additional reward is that if well designed a priori and approved by your institutional review board, the findings may be publishable as well. This is another opportunity for conducting research about your teaching and student learning that we referred to earlier as the Scholarship of Teaching and Learning (SoTL). Being a teacher-scholar means that you apply the same scholarly logic and methods of science to your classroom and teaching as you do the research in your sociological specialty.

Conclusion

We cannot say it loud enough or repeat it often enough—the goal of teaching is always to produce learning. Resources such as student course evaluations, peer reviews of teaching, classroom assessment techniques, and SoTL research findings provide faculty members with the opportunity to reflect upon their pedagogical practices and make improvements which can increase student learning as well as instructor effectiveness. While evaluation sometimes makes us uneasy, and perhaps may even be painful occasionally, the benefits that result from reflecting on the feedback we receive can enable us to develop our skills and repertoire as teachers who are focused on student learning!

CHAPTER TEN

~

The Importance of First Contact
in Introductory Sociology

The contexts in which we teach are many and diverse. In fact, the differentiation among institutions may be the most salient feature of American higher education (Calhoun 1999). If we are to take teaching and learning in sociology seriously, we must take these institutional differences and differences in the types of students we encounter seriously. Thus there is no single "correct" recipe for effective teaching in introductory sociology. Instead, the appropriate strategies depend upon our contexts and our audience. A well-designed and executed course on one campus may be completely inappropriate and ineffective on another. We have argued that we must design our courses to fit with the mission of our institution, the goals of our programs, and the learning objectives of the course.

There is a multitude of ways to be an effective teacher. However, there are also plenty of commonalities in good teaching that promote student learning. In this book, we have provided a step-by-step guide for the new or experienced teacher who is concerned with student learning and wants to have a successful first contact with students in introductory sociology. In sociology especially, the connections between our program goals, course goals, syllabi, and classroom activities frequently seem vague at best. Too often we have seen faculty members of the same department or program working without a consensual set of goals and purposes. We have argued that the various aspects of teaching discussed herein are closely connected parts of the same process—all of which are designed to aid student learning. When one aspect of this process is unconnected to the others, we provide a disservice to our students, who may have difficulty finding those connections on their own.

Unfortunately in higher education generally and in sociology specifically, faculty members often assume that curriculum and goals are matters for individual instructors rather than being "owned" by the faculty collectively. That collective ownership and responsibility means we must do the hard work of engaging in collegial discussions and debates regarding the nature of the curriculum, objectives, learning goals, and outcomes assessment in introductory sociology. We should also be discussing which pedagogical strategies can help us achieve those goals. When faculty members slight this process they are relinquishing their power to define curricula to others who will do it for us (e.g., administrators, publishers, textbook authors). We call for greater discussion and publication about teaching in general, teaching introductory sociology in particular, but especially about core principles fundamental to sociology and about how we present our discipline to the general public.

However, we are not calling for lockstep conformity in the way introductory sociology is taught. We believe that every faculty member brings his or her own strengths and styles to the classroom in ways that can be highly beneficial to student learning. In this book we have presented a variety of the most commonly used pedagogical strategies without trying to present a comprehensive review of all possible strategies—something which is beyond the scope of this project. To keep up to date on the very latest work on pedagogy, we recommend taking full advantage of the wide range of research on teaching and learning specific to sociology, such as articles that appear in the journal *Teaching Sociology* and the ASA's Teaching Resources and Innovations Library for Sociology (TRAILS). We are not recommending a stifling conformity, but we do stress the need for reflective dialogue among colleagues teaching introductory sociology addressing both the course and its role in the wider curriculum.

As committed educators we want to provide students with the very best learning experiences possible. As committed sociologists we want to provide our students with opportunities to see the beauty of our discipline, what it can do for their lives, and how sociology can provide tools to help make the world a better place. For most students, the introductory course will be the first and only contact they have with sociology. We have to step up to the challenge of facilitating the development of a sociological imagination in our students—to help them learn to see how biography and history impact their lives. If you teach students from a relatively privileged background, the challenge must be to help students recognize that society has bestowed on them more advantages relative to others. If your students face daily roadblocks to their success due to class, race, or gender, the challenge may be getting them to recognize those barriers so that they can be effectively addressed and students can be agents of change in their own lives as well as their communities. In any case, we need to help students see the relevance of sociology for making sense of their own experiences in society. When we have done so, we have succeeded in making effective first contact.

If we fail to make successful first contact with our students in this all-important introductory sociology course, then we fail at our purpose and we fail as ambassadors for our discipline. This is a much too important job for it to be taken for granted or relegated to the less committed or underprepared. The importance of this role also suggests that the very best faculty should be involved in teaching introductory sociology. It is not a job to be delegated only to those with weak institutional ties or the lowest levels of training. When we rely on part-time faculty or graduate students to help teach, we should also involve them in our ongoing discussion of the goals and objectives for the course and the broader curriculum. Connecting with students in introductory sociology or other first courses in sociology is the responsibility of each instructor who teaches this course. We must empower and involve *all* instructors if we are to rise to the challenge of effectively connecting with students, assisting their learning, preparing them for their world, and maybe even for preparing them for another course or two in sociology.

As we do so, we should systematically reflect upon our efforts through the scholarship of teaching and learning. As we research the level of effectiveness we attain in making first contact, we need to make those efforts public by sharing the results with others. This is public sociology at its finest! Sociologists, given our research training in both quantitative and qualitative strategies, are well positioned to conduct research on teaching and learning that is beneficial to our discipline and to higher education generally. We can also bring sociological concepts to the scholarship of learning and apply them to the classroom or other forms of instruction. We can help each other become teachers better able to facilitate our students' learning because we understand the dynamics of learning in a social context.

Effective teaching and learning is the best and biggest recruitment tool we have for our major and other programs. It's in our introductory courses that we recruit most majors to our discipline. It's in this context that we can strike a spark that may catch fire in our students as they learn to use their sociological imaginations. Helping our students to develop and use a sociological understanding of the world will make them better, more well-rounded citizens of the world whether or not they take another sociology course or become a sociology major. The opportunity of making first contact is a vitally important opportunity. We must maximize student opportunities to see why we love sociology the way that we do by being the very best teachers we can be. It is our hope that this book has contributed to your achievement of that goal and to a larger discussion about what we do in introductory sociology courses.

APPENDIX

~

Resources for Teaching and Learning in Introductory Sociology

The materials listed here are by no means a complete listing, but these resources may help you to build your library of pedagogical resources. Two major resources are the journal *Teaching Sociology* and publications available through the ASA bookstore (asanet.org).

Every issue of *Teaching Sociology* includes a wide range of articles that apply to teaching introductory sociology. A useful way to find articles of interest is to use the cumulative index for the journal, *Teaching Sociology: Twenty-Seven Year Index, 1973–1999*, compiled by Tara Burgess, Pauline Pavlakos, and Jeffrey Chin (2000). This index lists some 150 articles under the category "Introductory Sociology" and many more that relate to teaching introductory sociology in a variety of ways.

The ASA Bookstore is full of useful books, reports, and other documents helpful for curriculum development, teaching and learning, and assessment (asanet.org).

The Teaching Resources and Innovations Library for Sociology (TRAILS) which may be found at this site include syllabi, teaching techniques, assignments, etc. (asanet.org).

General Books on College Teaching

Teaching at Its Best: A Research-Based Resource for College Instructors, 2nd edition, by Linda B. Nilson, Jossey-Bass, 2010. This book, written by a sociologist, is a brief introduction to important topics in the design and teaching of a college course. It has a lot of practical information especially for the new teacher. Nilson does a good job of providing an overview of various teaching and learning techniques essential for the college instructor from syllabus construction to test preparation and everything in-between.

Teaching Tips: Strategies, Research, and Theory for College and University Teachers, 13th edition, by Marilla Svinicki and Wilbert J. McKeachie, Wadsworth, 2011. This excellent book covers a wide range of topics, including meeting the class for the first time, discussion, lecture, assessment and testing, cheating, grading, motivating students, writing, active learning, experiential learning, distance education, and ethics. Chapter 2 is a favorite: "Countdown for Course Preparation." In this chapter the authors talk about what to do three months before the first class (writing objectives, goals, or outcomes; choosing and ordering texts), two months, and one month before class, and finally, two weeks and one week before the first class.

These two books are out of print but may be found in the library:

Teaching Sociology: The Quest for Excellence, edited by Frederick L. Campbell, Hubert Blalock, Jr., and Reece McGee, Nelson-Hall, 1985. This book, written by some of today's master teachers in sociology, includes sections on barriers and constraints to teaching as well as essays by well-known sociologists about how to improve our teaching and the use of textbooks.

Passing on Sociology: The Teaching of a Discipline, by Charles Goldsmid and Everett K. Wilson, Wadsworth Publishing, 1980, reprinted by ASA, 1985. Available from the Teaching Resources Center of the ASA. This "definitive book" about teaching sociology is useful for current faculty, new teachers, and graduate students.

Books on Peer Review of Teaching

"Designing a Peer Review Observation Instrument," *Peer Review of Teaching*, edited by Carla Howery and Tom Van Valey, 2007.

Peer Review of Teaching: A Sourcebook, 2nd edition, by Nancy Van Note Chism and G. W. Chism, 2007. Boston: Anker.

Some Resources on Assessment, Curriculum Development, and Department Leadership

Assessing Student Learning in Sociology, edited by Charles S. Hohm and William S. Johnson. American Sociological Association, 2001.

Developing Outcomes-Based Assessment for Learner-Centered Education: A Faculty Introduction, by Amy Driscoll and Swarup Wood. Stylus Publishing, 2007.

Cultivating the Sociological Imagination: Concepts and Models for Service-Learning in Sociology, edited by James Ostrow, Gary Hesser, and Sandra Enos. Published by the American Association for Higher Education in cooperation with the ASA, 1999.

Distance and Cross-Campus Learning, edited by Meredith Redlin and Susan Hilal, 2003.

Included in Sociology: Learning Climates that Cultivate Racial and Ethnic Diversity, edited by Jeffrey Chin, Catherine White Berheide, and Dennis Rome. Published by the American Association for Higher Education in cooperation with the ASA, 2002.

Liberal Learning and the Sociology Major Updated: Meeting the Challenge of Teaching Sociology in the Twenty-First Century, by the ASA Task Force on the Undergraduate Major, K. McKinney, C. Howery, Kerry Strand, Edward Kain, and Catherine White Berheide. This ASA task force report provides recommendations for the undergraduate major. American Sociological Association, 2004 (asanet.org).

Sociology & General Education, by the ASA Task Force on Sociology and General Education. B. Keith, N. Greenwood, G. Hempe, H. Hartman, C. Howery, C. Jenkins, G. Kaufman, P. Meiksins, D. Reitzes, S. Ross, D. Swanson, and D. White. American Sociological Association, 2007 (asanet.org).

Service Learning and Undergraduate Sociology: Syllabi and Instructional Materials (2nd edition), edited by Brenda Marsteller Kowalewski, Morten G. Ender, and JoAnn DeFiore, 2001.

The Social World of Higher Education, edited by Bernice A. Pescosolido and Ronald Aminzade. Pine Forge Press, 1999. (Available at asanet.org.)

Teaching Sociology at Small Institutions, edited by Eric P. Godfrey, 1998.

Teaching Sociology in the Community College, edited by Maria I. Bryant, 1995.

Introductory Sociology Resource Manual, by James Sikora and Njeri Mbugua, ASA Teaching Resource Center, 2004 (e-book). The sixth edition contains eight articles about the core; twenty-one syllabi of introductory sociology courses; a wide array of assignments, projects, and class exercises; and a list of contributors. (Available at asanet.org.)

Groups

ASA Section on Teaching and Learning in Sociology offers workshops, SoTL sessions, and roundtables about teaching at every annual ASA meeting. You must be an ASA member to join, but section membership is affordable and you get a wonderful newsletter full of other interesting articles and news related to teaching and learning in sociology.

~

Bibliography

Agbetsiafa, Douglas. "Evaluating Effective Teaching in College Level Economics Using Student Ratings of Instruction: A Factor Analytic Approach." *Journal of College Teaching and Learning* 7, no. 5 (2010): 57–66.

Altman, H. B. and W. E. Cashin. "Idea Paper No. 27: Writing a Syllabus." Manhattan, KS: Center for Faculty Evaluation and Development, Kansas State University, 1992.

Angelo, Thomas A. and K. Patricia Cross. *Classroom Assessment Techniques: A Handbook for College Teachers.* San Francisco: Jossey-Bass, 1993.

Astin, Alexander W. *Achieving Educational Excellence.* San Francisco: Jossey-Bass, 1985.

Atwater, L. "Trading Places: Teaching with Students in the Center and Professors on the Periphery of the Principles Course." *Teaching Sociology* 19, no. 4 (1991): 483–88.

Auster, Carol J. and Mindy MacRone. "The Classroom as a Negotiated Social Setting: An Empirical Study of the Effects of Faculty Members' Behavior on Students' Participation." *Teaching Sociology* 22, no. 4 (1994): 289–300.

Babbie, Earl. "The Essential Wisdom of Sociology." *Teaching Sociology* 18, no. 4 (1990): 526–30.

Bain, Kenneth. "Evaluation of Teaching Using Student Ratings." (1996).

———. *What the Best College Teachers Do.* Cambridge, MA: Harvard University Press, 2004.

Baker, P. "Sociology Textbooks: Managing Clones or Writing Works of Distinction." *Teaching Sociology* 14, no. 4 (1988): 381–83.

Ballantine, Jeanne. "Course Analysis of Some Introductory Syllabi." In *Introductory Sociology: A Set of Syllabi and Related Materials*, edited by Charles Goldsmid, 5–7. Washington, D.C.: Teaching Resources Center, Section on Undergraduate Education, American Sociological Association, 1977.

———. "Discussion in Large Classes." In *Discussion in the College Classroom: Applications for Sociology Instruction*, edited by Jay R. Howard. Washington, D.C.: American Sociological Association, 2004.

———. "Introductory Teaching and Texts: How Did We Get into This Predicament?" *Teaching Sociology* 16, no. 4 (1988): 409–12.

Ballantine, Jeanne and Keith Roberts. *Our Social World*. 2nd edition. Los Angeles, CA: Pine Forge Press, 2009.

Barr, R. B. and John Tagg. "From Teaching to Learning—a New Paradigm for Undergraduate Education." *Change*, November/December 1995: 13–25.

Barry, Dave. *Dave Barry's Bad Habits: A 100% Fact-Free Book*. New York: Holt, 1993.

Beaudry, M. L. and T. Schaub. "The Learning-Centered Syllabus." *The Teaching Professor* 12, no. 2 (1998): 1–2.

Becker, A. and S. Calhoon. "What Introductory Psychology Students Attend to on a Course Syllabus." *Teaching of Psychology* 26, no. 1 (1999): 6–11.

Becker, H. S. and William C. Rau. "Sociology in the 1990s." *Choice*, November/December 1992.

Benton, Thomas H. "Remedial Civility Training." *The Chronicle of Higher Education* (2007), www.chronicle.com/article/.../56532/.

Bers, T. H., B. D. Davis, and B. Taylor. "The Use of Syllabi in Assessments: Unobtrusive Indicators and Tools for Faculty Development." *Assessment Update* 12, no. 3 (2000): 4–7.

Best, J. and D. Schweingruber. "First Words: Do Sociologists Actually Use the Terms in Introductory Sociology Textbooks' Glossaries?" *The American Sociologist* (Fall 2003): 97–106.

Biggs, John. *Teaching for Quality Learning at University*. Buckingham, UK: Open University Press, 1999.

Bligh, Donald A. *What's the Use of Lectures?* San Francisco: Jossey-Bass, 2000.

Bloom, B. S., ed. *The Taxonomy of Educational Objectives: Handbook I, Cognitive Domain*. New York: McKay, 1956.

Boersma, P. D., D. Gay, R. A. Jones, L. Morrison, and H. Remick. "Sex Differences in College Student-Teacher Interactions: Fact or Fantasy?" *Sex Roles* 7 (1981): 775–84.

Bok, Derek. *Our Underachieving Colleges*. Princeton, NJ: Princeton University Press, 2006.

Boyer, Ernest L. *Scholarship Reconsidered: Priority of the Professoriate*. Princeton, New Jersey: The Carnegie Foundation for the Advancement of Teaching, 1990.

Brookfield, Stephen D. and Stephen Preskill. *Discussion as a Way of Teaching: Tools and Techniques for Democratic Classrooms*. San Francisco, CA: Jossey-Bass, 1999.

Brooks, V. "Sex Differences in Student Dominance Behavior in Female and Male Professor's Classrooms." *Sex Roles* 8 (1982): 683–90.

Brown, George and Michael Manogue. "Refreshing Lecturing." *Medical Teacher* 23, no. 3 (2001): 231–44.

Burawoy, Michael. "2004 Presidential Address—for Public Sociology." *American Sociological Review* 70 (February 2005): 4–28.

Burgan, Mary. "In Defense of Lecturing." *Change* (November/December 2006): 31–34.

Calhoun, Craig. "The Changing Character of College: Institutional Transformation in American Higher Education." In *The Social Worlds of Higher Education: Handbook for Teaching in a New Century*, edited by Bernice A. Pescosolido and Ronald Aminzade, 9–31. Thousand Oaks, CA: Pine Forge, 1999.

Cannon, R. and David Newble. *A Handbook for Teachers in Universities and Colleges*. 4th ed. London: Kogan Page Limited, 2000.

Carl, John D. *Think Sociology*. Boston, MA: Pearson, 2000.

Cashin, W. E. "Student Ratings of Instruction: The Research Revisited, Idea Paper No. 32." Kansas State University Center for Faculty Evaluation and Development, 1995.

Charon, Joel. *Ten Questions: A Sociological Perspective*. 7th edition. Los Angeles: Wadsworth, 2009.

Chickering, Arthur W. and Zelda F. Gamson. "Seven Principles for Good Practice in Undergraduate Education." *The Wingspread Journal* (1987).

Chism, Nancy. *Peer Review of Teaching: A Sourcebook*. Boston, MA: Anker, 1999.

Chism, Nancy Van Note, and G. W. Chism. *Peer Review of Teaching: A Sourcebook*. 2nd ed. Bolton, MA: Anker, 2007.

Constantinople, Ann, Randolf Cornelius, and Janet M. Gray. "The Chilly Climate: Fact or Artifact?" *The Journal of Higher Education* 59 (1988): 526–50.

Cornelius, Randolf, Janet M. Gray, and Anne P. Constantinople. "Student Faculty Interaction in the College Classroom." *Journal of Research and Development in Education* 23 (1990): 189–97.

Cravens, Thomas F. "Students' Perceptions of the Characteristics of Teaching Excellence." (1996).

Crawford, Mary, and Margo MacLeod. "Gender in the College Classroom: An Assessment of the Chilly Climate for Women." *Sex Roles* 23 (1990): 101–22.

D'Antonio, William. "Nibbling at the Core." *Teaching Sociology* 10, no. 2 (1983): 169–85.

Davidovitch, Nitza and Dan Soen. "Myths and Facts about Student Surveys of Teaching and the Links between Students' Evaluations." *Journal of College Teaching and Learning* 6, no. 7 (2009): 41–50.

Davis, Brenda M. "Bored and Ignored or Gained and Maintained: Role of Attention in Beginning Class." *The Teaching Professor* 19, no. 6 (2005): 2.

Davis, James A. "Five Well-Established Research Results That I Think Are Probably True, Teachable in Introductory Sociology, and Worth Teaching." In *Teaching Sociology: The Quest for Excellence*, edited by F. Campbell, H. Blalock, Jr., R. McGee, 152-72. Chicago: Nelson-Hall, 1985.

deWinstanley, Patricia Ann and Robert A. Bjork. "Successful Lecturing: Presenting Information in Ways That Engage Effective Processing." *New Directions for Teaching and Learning* 89 (Spring 2002): 19–31.

DiBattista, David. "Fill-in-the-Blank Lecture Notes: Advantages." *The Teaching Professor* 19, no. 8 (2005): 1, 5.

Dominowski, Roger L. *Teaching Undergraduates*. London: Lawrence Erlbaum Associates, 2002.

Eberts, P., C. Howery, C. W. Berheide, K. Crittenden, R. Davis, Z. Gamson, and T. Wagenaar. *Liberal Learning and the Sociology Major: A Report to the Profession*. Washington, D.C.: American Sociological Association, 1991.

Eitzen, D. Stanley, Maxine Baca Zinn, and Kelly Eitzen Smith. *In Conflict and Order: Understanding Society*. 12th ed. New York: Pearson, 2010.

Erickson, B. LaSere. *Teaching College Freshmen*. San Francisco: Jossey-Bass, 1991.

Fassinger, Polly A. "Understanding Classroom Interaction: Students' and Professors' Contributions to Students' Silence." *The Journal of Higher Education* 66 (1995): 82–96.

Feldman, K. A. "Effective College Teaching from the Students' and Faculty View: Matched or Mismatched Priorities?" *Research in Higher Education* 28, no. 4 (1988): 291–344.

Filene, Peter. *The Joy of Teaching: A Practical Guide for New College Instructors*. Chapel Hill: University of North Carolina Press, 2005.

Friedman, N. L. "What Do We Really Teach in Introductory Sociology Textbooks? Three Underlying Messages and Their Instructional Implications." *The American Sociologist* (Summer 1991): 137–45.

Fritschner, Linda M. "Inside the Undergraduate College Classroom: Faculty and Students Differ on the Meaning of Student Participation." *The Journal of Higher Education* 71 (2000): 342–62.

Fry, E. "A Readability Formula That Saves Time." *Journal of Reading* 11 (1968): 513–16.

Garside, Colleen. "Look Who's Talking: A Comparison of Lecture and Group Discussion Teaching Activities in Developing Critical Thinking Skills." *Communication Education* 42 (1996): 212–27.

Geertsen, R. "The Textbook: An Acids Test." *Teaching Sociology* 5 (1977): 101–20.

Gerald, D. E. and W. J. Hussar. *Projections of Educational Statistics to 2012.* 31st ed. Washington, D.C.: U.S. Government Printing Office, 2002.

Gigliotti, Richard T. "Are They Getting What They Expect?" *Teaching Sociology* 15 (1987): 365–75.

Goldsmid, Charles A. "Why Formalize the Aims of Instruction?" *Teaching Sociology* 8 (1980): 263–90.

Goldsmid, C. A. and E. K. Wilson. *Passing on Sociology: The Teaching of a Discipline.* Belmont, CA: Wadsworth Publishing Company, 1980.

Graham, F. "Some Observations on Sociology Textbooks: An Editorial Perspective." *Teaching Sociology* 16, no. 4 (1988): 356–65.

Green, Charles S. III and Dean S. Dorn. "The Changing Classroom: The Meaning of Shifts in Higher Education for Teaching and Learning." In *The Social Worlds of Higher Education: Handbook for Teaching in a New Century,* edited by Bernice A. Pescosolido and Ronald Aminzade. Thousand Oaks, CA: Pine Forge, 1999.

Greenwood, Nancy A. and Margaret Cassidy. "A Critical Review of Family Sociology Textbooks." *Teaching Sociology* 18, no. 4 (1990): 541–49.

———. "A Review of Introductory Marriage and Family Texts: Standards for Evaluation." *Teaching Sociology* 14, no. 4 (1986): 295–302.

Hall, Roberta M. and Bernice R. Sandler. *The Classroom Climate: A Chilly One for Women? Project on the Status and Education of Women.* Washington, D.C.: Association for American Colleges, 1982.

Harp, Shannon F. and Amy Maslich. "The Consequences of Including Seductive Details During Lecture." *Teaching of Psychology* 32, no. 2 (2005): 100–03.

Harris, M. McDonnell. "Motivating with the Course Syllabus." *The National Teaching and Learning Forum* 3, no. 1 (1993): 1–3.

Hayes, Tom and Lesley Pugsley. "How to Produce Handouts." *Education for Primary Care* 17 (2006): 75–77.

Heller, Jack F., C. Richard Puff, and Carol J. Mills. "Assessment of the Chilly College Climate for Women." *The Journal of Higher Education* 56 (1985): 446–61.

Henslin, James E. *The Essentials of Sociology: A Down-to-Earth Approach.* New York: Pearson/Allyn and Bacon, 2008.

Hess, B. "In Defense of the Introductory Textbook." *Teaching Sociology* 16, no. 4 (1988): 403–04.

Heward, William L. "Guided Notes: Improving the Effectiveness of Your Lectures." http//ada.osu.edu/resources/fastfacts/Guided-Notes-Fact-Sheet .pdf, 2003.

hooks, bell. *Teaching to Transgress: Education as the Practice of Freedom.* New York: Routledge, 1994.

Howard, Jay R. "Do College Students Participate More in Discussion in Traditional Delivery Courses or in Interactive Telecourses? A Preliminary Comparison." *The Journal of Higher Education* 73, no. 6 (November/ December 2002): 64–780.

———. "An Examination of Student Learning in Introductory Sociology at a Commuter Campus." *Teaching Sociology* 33, no. 2 (2005): 195–205.

———. "What Does the Research Tell Us About Classroom Discussion?" In *Discussion in the College Classroom: Applications for Sociology Instruction,* edited by Jay R. Howard, 2–8. Washington, D.C.: American Sociological Association, 2004.

Howard, Jay R. and Roberta Baird. "The Consolidation of Responsibility and Students' Definitions of the College Classroom." *The Journal of Higher Education* 71 (2000): 700–21.

Howard, Jay R. and Amanda L. Henney. "Student Participation and Instructor Gender in the Mixed Aged College Classroom." *The Journal of Higher Education* 69 (1998): 384–405.

Howard, Jay R., George James, and David R. Taylor. "The Consolidation of Responsibility in the Mixed-Aged College Classroom." *Teaching Sociology* 30, no. 2 (2002): 214–34.

Howard, Jay R., Lillard B. Short, and Susan M. Clark. "Student Participation in the Mixed-Aged Classroom." *Teaching Sociology* 24 (1996): 8–24.

Howard, Jay R. and Aimee Zoellar. "The Role of the Introductory Sociology Course on Students' Perceptions of Achievement of General Educational Goals." *Teaching Sociology* 35, no. 3 (2007): 209–22.

Howard, Jay R., Aimee Zoeller, and Yale Pratt. "Students' Race and Participation in Classroom Discussion in Introductory Sociology: A Preliminary Investigation." *Journal of the Scholarship of Teaching and Learning* 6, no. 1 (2006): 14–38.

Huba, M. and J. E. Freed. "Understanding Hallmarks of Learner-Centered Teaching and Assessment." In *New Strategies in College Teaching: Succeeding in Today's Academic World*. Boston: Allyn and Bacon, 2002.

Jenkins, Carol A. "Plagiarism in a Multicultural Context: Implications for Teaching and Learning." In *Cross Paper #12*. Phoenix: League for Innovation in the Community College, 2009.

Jennings, Todd. "Teaching 'Out' in the University: An Investigation into the Effects of Lesbian, Bisexual, and Transgender Faculty Self-Disclosure upon Student Evaluations of Teaching Effectiveness in the USA." *International Journal of Inclusive Education* 14, no. 4 (2010): 325–39.

Johnson, David W., Roger T. Johnson, and Karl A. Smith. "Cooperative Learning: Increasing College Faculty Instructional Productivity." Washington, D.C.: ASHE ERIC Higher Education, 1991.

Jung, Jan, Rosemary L. Moore, and Jim Parker. "A Study of Older Students' Participation in the College Classroom." 1999.

Kammeyer, K. C. W. "Are Sociology Textbooks Really So Bad?" *Teaching Sociology* 16, no. 4 (1988): 424–27.

Karp, David A. and William C. Yoels. "The College Classroom: Some Observations on the Meaning of Student Participation." *Sociology and Social Research* 60 (1976): 421–39.

Katz, Joseph and Mildred Henry. *Turning Professors into Teachers*. New York: MacMillan, 1988.

Keith, Bruce and Morten G. Ender. "Core, What Core? Looking Beyond the Introductory Textbook for Answers." *Teaching Sociology* 32, no. 1 (2004b): 39–40.

———. "The Sociological Core: Conceptual Patterns and Idiosyncrasies in the Structure and Content of Introductory Sociology Textbooks, 1940–2000." *Teaching Sociology* 32, no. 1 (2004a): 19–26.

Keith, Bruce, Nancy A. Greenwood, Gary Hempe, Harriet Hartman, Carla B. Howery, Carol Jenkins, Gayle Kaufman, Peter Meiksins, Donald Reitzes, Susan Ross, Debra Swanson, and Deborah White (Task Force on Sociology and General Education). *Sociology and General Education*. Washington, D.C.: American Sociological Association, 2007.

Kember, David and Lyn Gow. "Orientations to Teaching and Their Effect on the Quality of Student Learning." *The Journal of Higher Education* 65 (1994): 58–74.

Kendall, Dianne. "Doing a Good Deed or Confounding the Problem? Peer Review and Sociology Textbooks." *Teaching Sociology* 27, no. 1 (1999): 17–30.

Kogan, Lori R., Regina Schoenfeld-Tacher, and Peter W. Hellyer. "Student Evaluations of Teaching: Perceptions of Faculty Based on Gender, Position, and Rank." *Teaching in Higher Education* 15, no. 6 (2010): 623–36.

Kuh, George D., Jillian Kinzie, Jennifer A. Buckley, Brian Bridges, and John C. Hayek. "What Matters to Student Success: A Review of the Literature." In *Commissioned Report for the National Symposium on Postsecondary Student Success: Spearheading a Dialog on Student Success*. National Postsecondary Education Cooperative, 2006.

Kuh, George D., Jillian Kinzie, John H. Schuh, Elizabeth J. Whitt, and Associates. *Student Success in College: Creating Conditions That Matter*. San Francisco, CA: Jossey-Bass, 2005.

Lang, James M. "Beyond Lecturing." *The Chronicle of Higher Education*, September 29, 2006 (http://chronicle.com/jobs/news/2006/09/2006092901/printable.html).

———. *On Course: A Week-by-Week Guide to Your First Semester of College Teaching*. Cambridge, MA: Harvard University Press, 2008.

Leamnson, Robert. *Thinking About Teaching and Learning: Developing Habits of Learning with First Year College and University Students*. Sterling, VA: Stylus, 1999.

Lemert, Charles. *Social Things: An Introduction to Social Life*. New York: Rowman and Littlefield, 2008.

Lenski, Gerhard. "Rethinking the Introductory Sociology Course." In *Teaching Sociology: The Quest for Excellence*, edited by Hubert M. Blalock, Fredrick Campbell, Jr., and Reece McGee. Chicago: Nelson-Hall, 1985.

Levine, Arthur. "How the Academic Profession Is Changing." In *The Social World of Higher Education: Handbook for Teaching in a New Century*, edited by Bernice A. Pescosolido and Ronald Aminzade, 42–53. Thousand Oaks, CA: Pine Forge, 1999.

Lewis, Jerry M. *Tips for Teaching Introductory Sociology*. Minneapolis/St. Paul: West Publishing, 1995.

Light, Richard J. *Making the Most of College: Students Speak Their Minds*. Cambridge, MA: Harvard University Press, 2001.

Lindahl, Mary W. and Michael L. Unger. "Cruelty in Student Teaching Evaluations." *College Teaching* 58, no. 3 (2010): 71–76.

Lindsey, L. and S. Beach. *Sociology*. 2nd ed. Upper Saddle River, NJ: Prentice Hall, 2002.

Lo, Celia C. "How Student Satisfaction Factors Affect Perceived Learning." *Journal of the Scholarship of Teaching and Learning* 10, no. 1 (2010): 47–54.

Lyons, R. E., M. McIntosh, and M. L. Kysilka. *Teaching College in an Age of Accountability*. Boston: Allyn and Bacon, 2003.

Macionis, John. *Sociology*. 9th ed. Upper Saddle River, NJ: Prentice Hall, 2003.

———. *Sociology*. 13th ed. New York: Pearson, 2010.

Madison, James H. "Teaching with Images." *OAH Magazine of History* (January 2004), 65–68.

McGee, R. "Determining Course Content in the Introductory Course." *Teaching Sociology* 22 (October 1994): 345–50.

———. "The Sociology of Sociology Textbooks." In *Teaching Sociology: A Quest for Excellence*, edited by F. Campbell, H. Blalock, Jr., and R. McGee, 175–201. Chicago: Nelson-Hall, 1985.

———, ed. *Teaching the Mass Class*. 2nd ed. Washington D.C.: American Sociological Association Teaching Resource Center, 1991.

McKeachie, Wilbert J. *McKeachie's Teaching Tips: Strategies, Research and Theory for College and University Teachers*. 11th ed. College Teaching Series. Boston: Houghton Mifflin Company, 2002.

———. "Research on College Teaching: The Historical Background." *Journal of Educational Psychology* 82 (1990): 189–200.

———. *Teaching Tips: A Guidebook for the Beginning College Teacher*. 7th ed: Lexington, MA: D. C. Heath and Company, 1978.

———. *Teaching Tips: A Guidebook for the Beginning College Teacher*. 9th ed. Lexington, MA: D. C. Heath, 1994.

McKinney, Kathleen and Barbara S. Heyl, ed. *Sociology through Active Learning: Student Exercises*. 2nd ed. Los Angeles, CA: Pine Forge Press, 2009.

McKinney, Kathleen, Carla Howery, Kerry J. Strand, Edward L. Kain, and Catherine White Berheide. *Liberal Learning and the Sociology Major Updated: Meeting the Challenge of Teaching Sociology in the Twenty-First Century*. Washington, D.C.: American Sociological Association, 2004.

McLaughlin, Kevin and Henry Mandin. "A Schematic Approach to Diagnosing and Resolving Lecturalgia." *Medical Education* 35 (2001): 1135–42.

Mentkowski, Marcia and Associates. *Learning That Lasts: Integrating Learning, Development, and Performance in College and Beyond*. San Francisco, CA: Jossey-Bass, 2005.

Mills, C. Wright. *The Sociological Imagination*. Oxford: Oxford University Press, 1959.

Morgan, C. H., J. D. Lilley, and N. C. Boreham. "Learning from Lectures: The Effect of Varying Detail in the Lecture Handouts on Notetaking and Recall." *Applied Cognitive Psychology* 2 (1988): 115–22.

Neer, Michael R. and W. Faye Kircher. "Apprehensives' Perceptions of Classroom Factors Influencing Their Class Participation." *Communication Research Reports* 6 (1989): 70–77.

Nilson, Linda B. *Teaching at Its Best: A Research-Based Resource for College Instructors*. 3rd ed. San Francisco: Jossey-Bass, 2010.

Nolan, Patrick and Gerhard Lenski. *Human Societies: An Introduction to Macrosociology*. Boulder, CO: Paradigm Publishers, 2008.

Novak, G. M., E. Patterson, A. Gavrin, and W. Christian. *Just-in-Time Teaching: Blending Active Learning with Web Technologies*. Upper Saddle River, NJ: Prentice-Hall, 1999.

Nunn, Claudia E. "Discussion in the College Classroom: Triangulating Observational and Survey Results." *The Journal of Higher Education* 67 (1996): 243–66.

Parkes, J. and M. B. Harris. "The Purposes of a Syllabus." *College Teaching* 50, no. 2 (2002): 55–61.

Pearson, Judy and Richard West. "An Initial Investigation of the Effects of Gender on Student Questions in the Classroom: Developing a Descriptive Base." *Communication Education* 40 (1991): 22–32.

Perrucci, Robert. "The Failure of Excellence in Texts." In *Teaching Sociology: A Quest for Excellence*, edited by F. Campbell, H. Blalock, Jr., and R. McGee. Chicago: Nelson-Hall, 1985.

Persell, C. Hodges. "Reflections on Sociology Textbooks by a Teacher, Scholar, and Author." *Teaching Sociology* 16, no. 4 (1988): 399–402.

Persell, C. Hodges, Kathryn May Pfeiffer, and Ali Syed. "What Should Students Understand after Taking Introduction to Sociology?" *Teaching Sociology* 35 (October 2007): 1–15.

Poon, L. W. "Learning." In *The Encyclopedia of Aging*, edited by G. L. Maddox. New York: Springer, 1995.

Ragan, James F. Jr. and Bhavneet Walia. "Differences in Student Evaluations of Principles and Other Economics Courses and the Allocation of Faculty across Courses." *Journal of Economic Education* 41, no. 4 (2010): 335–52.

Raymark, P. H. and P. A. Connor-Greene. "The Syllabus Quiz." *Teaching of Psychology* 29, no. 4 (2002): 286–88.

Roberts, Keith. "Beyond Content: Deep-Structure Objectives for Sociology and Social Science Curricula." In *Sea-Changes in Social Science Education*, edited by Charles S. White. Boulder, CO: Social Science Education Consortium, 2001.

———. "Sociology in the General Education Curriculum: A Cognitive Structuralist Perspective." *Teaching Sociology* 14 (October 1986): 207–16.

Royce, D. "Basic Course Components." In *New Strategies in College Teaching*, 84–107. Boston: Allyn and Bacon, 2002.

Rubin, S. "Professors, Students and the Syllabus." in *Field Guide for Teaching in a New Century*, edited by B. Pescosolido and R. Aminzade, 1999.

Schaefer, Richard T. *Sociology*. 11th ed. New York: McGraw-Hill, 2010.

——. *Sociology Matters*. New York: McGraw-Hill, 2011.

——. "Textbooks: The Responsibilities of the Author, Publisher and Instructor." *Teaching Sociology* 16, no. 4 (1988): 396–98.

Schaie, K. W. "Abilities." In *The Encyclopedia of Aging*, edited by G. L. Maddox. New York: Springer, 1995.

Sikora, James and Njeri Mbugua. *Introductory Sociology Resource Manual*. 6th ed. Washington, D.C.: American Sociological Association, 2004.

Simonton, D. "Creativity and Wisdom in Aging." In *Handbook of the Psychology of Aging*, edited by J. Birren and K. W. Schaie, 320–29. New York: Academic Press, 1990.

Smith, Bettye P. "Student Ratings of Teaching Effectiveness: An Analysis of End-of-Course Faculty Evaluations." *College Student Journal* 41, no. 4 (2007): 788–800.

Smith, C. B. "Sociology and the Liberal Arts: A Socio-Historical Integration." *Teaching Sociology* 18 (October 1990): 482–87.

Smith, Daryl G. "College Classroom Interactions and Critical Thinking." *Journal of Educational Psychology* 69 (1977): 180–90.

Smith, R. A. "Preventing Lost Syllabi." *Teaching of Psychology* 20, no. 2 (1993): 113.

Snyder, Thomas D., Sally A. Dillow, and Charlene M. Hoffman. "Chapter Three: Post Secondary Education." In *Digest of Educational Statistics 2008*, 266 and 457. Washington, D.C.: National Center for Education Statistics, Institute of Educational Sciences, U.S. Department of Education, 2009.

Statham, A., L. Richardson, and J. A. Cook. *Gender and University Teaching: A Negotiated Difference*. Albany, NY: State University of New York (SUNY), 1991.

Sternglanz, Sarah Hall and Shirley Lyberger-Ficek. "Sex Differences in Student-Teacher Interactions in the College Classroom." *Sex Roles* 3 (1977): 345–52.

Svinicki, Marilla and Wilbert J. McKeachie. *McKeachie's Teaching Tips: Strategies, Research, and Theory for College and University Teachers*. 13th ed. Belmont, CA: Wadsworth, 2010.

Szafran, R. F. "What Do Introductory Sociology Students Know and When Do They Know It? The Results of Pretesting Students." *Teaching Sociology* 14, no. 4 (1986): 217–23.

Tinto, Vincent. "Classrooms as Communities: Exploring the Educational Character of Student Persistence." *The Journal of Higher Education* 68 (1997): 599–623.

Trigwell, Keith, Michael Prosser, and Fiona Waterhouse. "Relations between Teachers' Approaches to Teaching and Students' Approaches to Learning." *Higher Education* 37 (1997): 57–70.

Wagenaar, Theodore C. "Assessing Sociological Knowledge: A First Try." *Teaching Sociology* 32, no. 2 (2004b): 232–38.

———. "Goals for the Discipline?" *Teaching Sociology* 19, no. 1 (1991): 92–95.

———. "Is There a Core in Sociology? Results from a Survey." *Teaching Sociology* 32, no. 1 (2004a): 1–18.

Weast, Don. "Alternative Teaching Strategies: The Case for Critical Thinking." *Teaching Sociology* 24 (1996): 189–94.

Weimer, Maryellen. *Improving Your Classroom Teaching*. In *Survival Skills for Scholars*, edited by Mitch Allen. Newbury Park: Sage Publications, 1993.

———. *Learning-Centered Teaching: Five Key Changes to Practice*. San Francisco: Jossey-Bass, 2002.

Westhues, K. "Transcending the Textbook World." *Teaching Sociology* 19, no. 1 (1991): 87–92.

Wilson, E. K. "A Checklist for Reviewing Syllabi." In *Introductory Sociology Resource Manual*, edited by K. McKinney and J. Sikora, 5–6. Washington, D.C.: Teaching Resources Center, American Sociological Association, 1990.

Young, Jeffery R. "How Social Networking Helps Teaching (and Worries Some Professors)." *The Chronicle of Higher Education*, July 22, 2010.

———. "Student's Political Awareness Hits Highest Level in a Decade." *The Chronicle of Higher Education*, January 30, 2004, 30–32.

Names Index

Subject Index